The Original
Summer Bridge Activities™

Bridging Grades Sixth to Seventh

Caution: Exercise activities may require adult supervision. Before beginning any exercise activity, consult a physician. Written parental permission is suggested for those using this book in group situations. Children should always warm up prior to beginning any exercise activity and should stop immediately if they feel any discomfort during exercise.

Caution: Before beginning any food activity, ask parents' permission and inquire about the child's food allergies and religious or other food restrictions.

Caution: Nature activities may require adult supervision. Before beginning any nature activity, ask parents' permission and inquire about the child's plant and animal allergies. Remind the child not to touch plants or animals during the activity without adult supervision.

The authors and publisher are not responsible or liable for any injury that may result from performing the exercises or activities in this book.

Credits

Series Creator: Michele D. Van Leeuwen

Content Editor: JulieAnna Kirsch

Copy Editor: Deborah Prato

Layout and Cover Design: Chasity Rice

Cover Illustration: Robbie Short

ISBN 978-1-60418-823-3

Table of Contents

About Summer Learning

Dear Parents:

Did you know that many children experience learning loss when they do not engage in educational activities during the summer? This means that some of what they have spent time learning over the preceding school year evaporates during the summer months. However, summer learning loss is something that you can help prevent. Below are a few suggestions for fun and engaging activities that can help children maintain and grow their academic skills during the summer.

- Read with your child every day. Visit your local library together and select books on subjects that interest your child.

- Ask your child's teacher to recommend books for summer reading.

- Explore parks, nature preserves, museums, and cultural centers.

- Consider every day as a day full of teachable moments. Measuring ingredients for recipes and reviewing maps before a car trip are ways to learn or reinforce skills.

- Each day, set goals for your child to accomplish. For example, complete five math problems or read one section or chapter in a book.

- Encourage your child to complete the activities in books such as Summer Bridge Activities™ to help bridge the summer learning gap.

To learn more about summer learning loss and summer learning programs, visit *www.summerlearning.org.*

Have a memorable summer!

Ron Fairchild

CEO, National Summer Learning Association

About Summer Bridge Activities™

Summer Bridge Activities™: Bridging Grades Sixth to Seventh helps prepare your rising seventh grader for a successful school year. The activities in this book are designed to review the skills that your child mastered in sixth grade, preview the skills that he or she will learn in seventh grade, and help prevent summer learning loss. No matter how wonderful your child's classroom experiences are, your involvement outside the classroom is crucial to his or her academic success. Together with *Summer Bridge Activities™: Bridging Grades Sixth to Seventh*, you can fill the summer months with learning experiences that will deepen and enrich your child's knowledge and prepare your child for the upcoming school year.

Summer Bridge Activities™ is the original workbook series developed to help parents support their children academically during the summer months. While many other summer workbook series are available, Summer Bridge Activities™ continues to be the series that teachers recommend most.

The three sections in this workbook correspond to the three months of traditional summer vacation. Each section begins with a goal-setting activity, a word list, and information about the fitness and character development activities located throughout the section.

To achieve maximum results, your child should complete two activity pages each day. Each activity page is numbered by day, and activities cover a range of subjects, including reading comprehension, writing, grammar, fractions, geometry, social studies, science, and fitness. These grade-appropriate activities are presented in a fun and creative way to challenge and engage your child.

Bonus extension activities that encourage outdoor learning, science experiments, and social studies exercises are located at the end of each section. Complete these activities with your child throughout each month as time allows.

An answer key located at the end of the book allows you to check your child's work. The included flash cards help reinforce basic skills, and a certificate of completion will help you and your child celebrate his or her summer learning success!

Skills Matrix

Day	Addition & Subtraction	Algebra & Ratios	Capitalization & Punctuation	Character Development	Data Analysis & Probability	Decimals & Percentages	Fitness	Fractions	Geometry & Measurement	Language Arts	Multiplication & Division	Parts of Speech	Problem Solving	Puzzles	Reading Comprehension	Science	Sentence Types & Structure	Social Studies	Usage	Writing
1	★									★	★					★	★			
2								★		★							★	★		
3			★					★							★					
4								★		★							★			★
5							★	★		★			★				★			
6								★							★					
7								★		★				★			★			
8								★		★						★	★			
9								★							★		★			
10				★				★		★		★								
11								★		★		★						★		
12								★		★		★								★
13								★				★			★					
14										★		★	★							★
15							★	★		★		★								
16								★				★			★					
17								★		★		★						★		
18								★		★		★				★				
19								★				★			★					
20								★				★	★	★						★
BONUS PAGES!				★												★		★		
1										★		★	★		★					
2								★				★			★					
3								★		★		★				★				
4							★	★		★		★								
5								★				★			★					
6					★					★		★								★
7					★					★		★				★				
8					★							★			★					
9				★						★		★	★							
10					★					★		★			★					
11					★							★			★					

Skills Matrix

Day	Addition & Subtraction	Algebra & Ratios	Capitalization & Punctuation	Character Development	Data Analysis & Probability	Decimals & Percentages	Fitness	Fractions	Geometry & Measurement	Language Arts	Multiplication & Division	Parts of Speech	Problem Solving	Puzzles	Reading Comprehension	Science	Sentence Types & Structure	Social Studies	Usage	Writing
12						★		★		★		★								★
13						★	★	★		★		★								
14						★		★				★			★					
15						★						★			★	★				
16						★						★			★			★		
17						★						★			★					
18		★								★		★					★			
19		★								★									★	★
20		★													★		★			
BONUS PAGES!									★	★						★		★		★
1					★					★							★			★
2					★					★					★					★
3			★										★		★					
4			★		★		★			★										
5			★		★					★						★				
6			★										★		★					
7	★		★							★								★		
8	★		★							★										★
9	★		★												★					
10			★						★	★						★				
11			★						★	★						★				
12			★							★					★					
13			★	★						★	★									
14			★							★				★						★
15			★							★					★					
16										★					★	★			★	
17			★				★			★	★									
18			★							★					★					
19			★							★					★					★
20										★			★				★	★		
BONUS PAGES!																★		★		★

Encouraging Summer Reading

Literacy is the single most important skill that your child needs to be successful in school. The following list includes ideas of ways that you can help your child discover the great adventures of reading!

- Establish a time for reading each day. Ask your child about what he or she is reading. Try to relate the material to an event that is happening this summer or to another book or story.

- Let your child see you reading for enjoyment. Talk about the great things that you discover when you read.

- Create a summer reading list. Choose books from the reading list (pages ix–x) or head to the library and explore the shelves. A general rule for selecting books at the appropriate reading level is to choose a page and ask your child to read it aloud. If he or she does not know more than five words on the page, the book may be too difficult.

- Read newspaper and magazine articles, recipes, menus, and maps on a daily basis to show your child the importance of reading.

- Find books that relate to your child's experiences. For example, if you are going camping, find a book about camping. This will help your child develop new interests.

- Visit the library each week. Let your child choose his or her own books but do not hesitate to ask your librarian for suggestions. Often, librarians can recommend books based on what your child enjoyed in the past.

- Make up stories. This is especially fun to do in the car, on camping trips, or while waiting at the airport. Encourage your child to tell a story with a beginning, a middle, and an end. Or, have your child start a story and let other family members build on it.

- Encourage your child to join a summer reading club at the library or a local bookstore. Your child may enjoy talking to other children about the books that he or she has read.

Summer Reading List

The summer reading list includes fiction and nonfiction titles. Experts recommend that students entering seventh grade read for at least 30 minutes each day. Then, you should ask your child questions about the story to reinforce comprehension.

Decide on an amount of daily reading time for each month. You may want to have your child write the time on the Monthly Goals page at the beginning of each section.

Fiction

Anderson, Laurie Halse
Fever 1793

Armstrong, William H.
Sounder

Balliett, Blue
Chasing Vermeer

Bloor, Edward
Tangerine

Blumberg, Rhoda
Commodore Perry in the Land of the Shogun

Blume, Judy
Starring Sally J. Freedman as Herself

Byars, Betsy
The Pinballs

Clement-Davies, David
Fire Bringer

Creech, Sharon
Chasing Redbird

Curtis, Christopher Paul
Bud, Not Buddy

Denenberg, Barry
Mirror, Mirror on the Wall: The Diary of Bess Brennan, The Perkins School for the Blind, 1932

Edwards, Julie Andrews
The Last of the Really Great Whangdoodles

Fast, Howard
April Morning

Fleischman, Sid
The Whipping Boy

Fritz, Jean
Homesick: My Own Story

Gutman, Dan
Jackie & Me

Hansen, Joyce
I Thought My Soul Would Rise and Fly: The Diary of Patsy, a Freed Girl, Mars Bluff, South Carolina, 1865

Hesse, Karen
Out of the Dust

Hiaasen, Carl
Flush
Hoot

Hobbs, Will
Go Big or Go Home

Holm, Jennifer L.
Our Only May Amelia

Joinson, Carla
A Diamond in the Dust

Summer Reading List (continued)

Fiction (continued)

Koller, Jackie French
Nothing to Fear

Konigsburg, E. L.
*From the Mixed-Up Files of
    Mrs. Basil E. Frankweiler*

McKinley, Robin
The Blue Sword

Montgomery, Lucy Maud
Anne of Green Gables

Myers, Walter Dean
The Outside Shot

Nelson, Theresa
The Empress of Elsewhere

Nye, Naomi Shihab
Habibi

O'Dell, Scott
The Black Pearl
The King's Fifth

Paulsen, Gary
The River

Rankin, Louise
Daughter of the Mountains

Rawls, Wilson
Where the Red Fern Grows

Rockwell, Thomas
How to Eat Fried Worms

Rowling, J. K.
Harry Potter and the Sorcerer's Stone

Snicket, Lemony
The Bad Beginning or, Orphans!

Speare, Elizabeth George
The Sign of the Beaver

Stewart, Trenton Lee
The Mysterious Benedict Society

Tolkien, J. R. R.
The Hobbit

Van Draanen, Wendelin
The Gecko and Sticky: Villain's Lair

Van Leeuwen, Jean
Bound for Oregon

Walsh, Jill Paton
The Green Book

Wilder, Laura Ingalls
Little House on the Prairie

Nonfiction

Curlee, Lynn
Skyscraper

Donald, Rhonda Lucas
Endangered Animals

Eckert, Allan W.
Incident at Hawk's Hill

Gutman, Bill
Lance Armstrong: A Biography

Murphy, Glenn
Inventions

Nelson, Kadir
*We Are the Ship: The Story of Negro
    League Baseball*

Walker, Niki
Generating Wind Power

Monthly Goals

A goal is something that you want to accomplish and must work toward. Sometimes, reaching a goal can be difficult.

Think of three goals to set for yourself this month. For example, you may want to exercise for 30 minutes each day. Write your goals on the lines. Post them someplace visible, where you will see them every day.

Place a check mark next to each goal that you complete. Feel proud that you have met your goals and set new ones to continue to challenge yourself.

1. _____

2. _____

3. _____

Word List

The following words are used in this section. Use a dictionary to look up each word that you do not know. Then, write three sentences. Use at least one word from the word list in each sentence.

conservation	radiocarbon dating
cuneiform	renovated
erosion	schedule
gridiron	sediment
polyps	tempo

1. _____

_____

2. _____

_____

3. _____

_____

Introduction to Flexibility

This section includes fitness and character development activities that focus on flexibility. These activities are designed to get you moving and thinking about building your physical fitness and your character.

Physical Flexibility

To the average person, *flexibility* means being able to accomplish everyday physical tasks easily, like bending to tie a shoe. These everyday tasks can be difficult for people whose muscles and joints have not been used and stretched regularly.

Proper stretching allows muscles and joints to move through their full range of motion, which is important for good flexibility. There are many ways that you stretch every day without realizing it. When you reach for a dropped pencil or a box of cereal on the top shelf, you are stretching your muscles. Flexibility is important to your health and growth, so challenge yourself to improve your flexibility consciously. Simple stretches and activities, such as yoga and tai chi, can improve your flexibility. Set a stretching goal for the summer, such as practicing daily until you can touch your toes.

Flexibility of Character

While it is important to have a flexible body, it is also important to be mentally flexible. Being mentally flexible means being open-minded to change. It can be disappointing when things do not go your way, but this is a normal reaction. Think of a time recently when unforeseen circumstances ruined your plans. Maybe your mother had to work one weekend, and you could not go to a baseball game with friends because you needed to babysit a younger sibling. How did you deal with this situation?

A large part of being mentally flexible is realizing that there will be situations in life where unforeseen things happen. Often, it is how you react to the circumstances that affects the outcome. Arm yourself with tools to be flexible, such as having realistic expectations, brainstorming solutions to make a disappointing situation better, and looking for good things that may result from the initial disappointment.

Mental flexibility can take many forms. For example, being fair, respecting the differences of other people, and being compassionate are ways that you can practice mental flexibility. In difficult situations, remind yourself to be flexible, and you will reap the benefits of this important character trait.

Solve each problem.

1. $3,281$
    $+ 1,952$

2. 23.25
    $+ 9.75$

3. $62,523$
    $- 13,145$

4. 66.7
    $- 1.954$

5. 483
    $\times 367$

6. $3,135$
    $\times 789$

7. 0.92
    $\times 1.5$

8. 4.18
    $\times 37$

9. $6\overline{)9,468}$

10. $7\overline{)2,307}$

11. $8\overline{)10.4}$

12. $4\overline{)2.6}$

Write C on the line if the group of words is a complete sentence. Write F if the group of words is a sentence fragment.

13. _____ I plan to be there before anyone else.

14. _____ If you go camping, be sure to take a warm sleeping bag.

15. _____ Behind the barn.

16. _____ When the game ended.

17. _____ Jumped over the puddle of water.

18. _____ Kareem helped his mom make dinner.

19. _____ Maggie found her key.

20. _____ The white owl on the tree branch.

DAY 1

Use the prefixes and suffixes and their meanings to write a definition for each word below.

Prefixes	Suffixes
re—back or again	ment—the act, result, or product of
dis—away, apart, or the opposite of	less—without or not
un—opposite, not, or lack of	
pre—before	

21. punishment _____

22. disappear_____

23. presoak _____

24. rewind _____

25. colorless _____

26. unsure _____

The scientific method is the process that scientists use when conducting experiments. Write the number of each step in the scientific method next to its description.

Step 1: Ask a Question   Step 2: Research the Topic

Step 3: Construct a Hypothesis   Step 4: Test and Observe

Step 5: Analyze and Draw Conclusions   Step 6: Report the Results

_____ A scientist studies the results and compares them to the original hypothesis.

_____ A scientist conducts the experiment, observes the results, and takes careful notes.

_____ A scientist asks *who, what, when, where,* and *why* about the topic.

_____ A scientist makes an informed prediction about the experiment's results.

_____ A scientist learns as much as possible about the topic.

_____ A scientist shares her hypothesis, method, and results with other scientists.

FACTOID: Antarctic ice is more than 2.6 miles (4.2 km) thick in some places.

Write the missing fractions on each number line.

1.

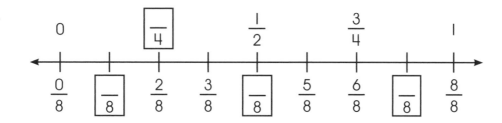

2.

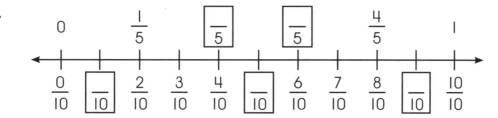

Write *C* on the line if the group of words is a complete sentence. Write *F* if the group of words is a sentence fragment. Write *R* if the group of words is a run-on sentence.

3. _____ The jockey mounted his horse.

4. _____ Whether there is enough food or not.

5. _____ We go swimming in the lake every summer it is always a lot of fun.

6. _____ We enjoyed the music.

7. _____ Loaned her favorite shirt to Alice.

Rewrite each sentence fragment as a complete sentence.

8. From high atop the stadium.

_____

_____

9. Hidden under the basket.

_____

_____

DAY 2

Circle the letter in front of the correct meaning for each root word. Then, write two words that contain the root word.

10. **bio**   A.   sea   B.   far   C.   life

_____ _____

11. **pend**   A.   one   B.   before   C.   hang

_____ _____

12. **path**   A.   feeling   B.   fear   C.   all

_____ _____

13. **chron**   A.   time   B.   fear   C.   study of

_____ _____

14. **port**   A.   carry   B.   out   C.   in

_____ _____

On the left is a list of things that people in a society need. On the right is a list of services that a government may provide to meet those needs. Match each government service with a need by writing the letter on the line.

15. _____ education

16. _____ communication

17. _____ safety

18. _____ protection

19. _____ transportation

20. _____ health

21. _____ help for the needy

22. _____ clean air and water

23. _____ money to trade for goods

A. printing money

B. building roads

C. funding and staffing public schools

D. providing a military

E. setting and enforcing speed limits

F. delivering mail

G. making laws to restrict pollution

H. building low-income housing

I. inspecting food and drugs

FITNESS FLASH: Touch your toes 10 times.

* See page ii.

Write two equivalent fractions for each fraction.

1. $\dfrac{2}{4}$ = ___ = ___   2. $\dfrac{2}{12}$ = ___ = ___   3. $\dfrac{8}{14}$ = ___ = ___   4. $\dfrac{4}{18}$ = ___ = ___

5. $\dfrac{10}{24}$ = ___ = ___   6. $\dfrac{4}{9}$ = ___ = ___   7. $\dfrac{10}{20}$ = ___ = ___   8. $\dfrac{18}{24}$ = ___ = ___

Complete each equivalent fraction.

9. $\dfrac{1}{11} = \dfrac{}{33}$ 10. $\dfrac{1}{4} = \dfrac{}{20}$ 11. $\dfrac{4}{16} = \dfrac{}{32}$ 12. $\dfrac{8}{9} = \dfrac{}{54}$

13. $\dfrac{3}{15} = \dfrac{}{45}$ 14. $\dfrac{2}{6} = \dfrac{}{36}$ 15. $\dfrac{5}{16} = \dfrac{}{48}$ 16. $\dfrac{3}{8} = \dfrac{}{24}$

Correct the paragraph. Look for errors in capitalization and punctuation.

Plate Tectonics

Earth's crust is broken into huge pieces called tectonic plates these plates include whole continents and sections of the ocean floor. Tectonic plates. Are shifting constantly. The uneven line where two plates meet is called a rift zone earthquakes often occur along rift zones. When part of a slowly moving plate. Sticks to an opposing plate at a point along the rift zone, pressure builds. The pressure rises behind the section until finally it gives way and moves The shock from this sudden shift is like a stone tossed into a pond It sends waves in all directions

DAY 3

Read the passage. Then, answer the questions.

Energy Conservation

Energy conservation means being careful about how much energy you use and trying to use less energy. You can conserve energy by driving cars with higher fuel efficiency, which means you can travel farther using less fuel. You can recycle or reuse materials, such as plastic, glass, paper, and metal, and you can buy products made from recycled materials. You can also conserve energy by using less at home. Wear heavier clothing instead of turning up the heat when the weather gets colder. Turn off the lights when you leave a room and unplug small appliances and machines, such as televisions and computers, when you will be away for a long period of time. Using less electricity, gas, and water means you will have lower utility bills, and you will help the environment.

17. What is the main idea of this passage?
    A. Some materials can be recycled instead of thrown away.
    B. Utility bills are sometimes higher in the summer.
    C. There are many ways to conserve energy.

18. What does the phrase *energy conservation* mean? _____

    _____

    _____

19. Why might you want to use a car with high fuel efficiency? _____

    _____

20. What are some materials that can be recycled? _____

    _____

    _____

21. What are two ways that you can help conserve energy at home? _____

    _____

    _____

    _____

FACTOID: Global temperatures have risen 1.4°F (0.8°C) since 1880.

Find the greatest common factor (GCF) for each pair of numbers.

1.   6   2.   15   3.   24

       18   20   32

      GCF: GCF: GCF:

4.   14   5.   14   6.   9

       21   35   15

      GCF: GCF: GCF:

7.   18   8.   4   9.   15

       27   12   40

      GCF: GCF: GCF:

Read each sentence. Write *D* on the line if the sentence is declarative. Write *INT* if the sentence is interrogative. Write *IMP* if the sentence is imperative. Write *E* if the sentence is exclamatory. Then, write the correct punctuation mark at the end of each sentence.

10. _____ Living in this city is so exciting

11. _____ Please repeat what you said earlier

12. _____ What an amazing performance Jamie gave

13. _____ Miguel started playing golf at a young age

14. _____ Will you pass the peas, please

15. _____ Lay your pencil down when you are finished

16. Rewrite one declarative sentence from above so that it is interrogative.

_____

_____

17. Rewrite one exclamatory sentence from above so that it is declarative.

_____

_____

DAY 4

Circle the letter in front of the correct meaning for each root word. Then, write two words that contain the root word.

18. **therm**   A. above   B. heat   C. after

_____   _____

19. **aud**   A. sound   B. for   C. taste

_____   _____

20. **morph**   A. love   B. form   C. change

_____   _____

21. **biblio**   A. form   B. good   C. book

_____   _____

22. **geo**   A. earth   B. measure   C. power

_____   _____

Imagine that you are in charge of making a new television show that combines all of the characters from your two favorite shows. What would happen in the first episode of your new show? Use another sheet of paper if you need more space.

_____

_____

_____

_____

_____

_____

_____

_____

_____

 FITNESS FLASH: Do 10 shoulder shrugs.

* See page ii.

DAY 5

Write each fraction in its simplest form.

1. $\dfrac{4}{6} =$

2. $\dfrac{5}{10} =$

3. $\dfrac{9}{15} =$

4. $\dfrac{8}{14} =$

5. $\dfrac{3}{15} =$

6. $\dfrac{6}{21} =$

7. $\dfrac{28}{42} =$

8. $\dfrac{22}{30} =$

9. $\dfrac{16}{32} =$

10. $\dfrac{35}{50} =$

Solve each problem. Simplify if possible.

11. A medium pizza was cut into 10 equal slices. Eight slices of pizza were eaten. Write a fraction to show how much pizza was eaten.

12. An extra-large pepperoni pizza was cut into 16 equal slices. A total of 10 slices of pizza were eaten. What fraction of the pizza was left?

Read each sentence. Write _D_ on the line if the sentence is declarative. Write _INT_ if the sentence is interrogative. Write _IMP_ if the sentence is imperative. Write _E_ if the sentence is exclamatory. Then, write the correct punctuation mark at the end of each sentence.

13. _____ Did you get to see Will's performance

14. _____ I love my baby sister so much

15. _____ Logan e-mailed an invitation to Yasmin

16. _____ What a beautiful ship it was

17. _____ Please answer the phone

18. _____ I am so glad you are coming to my piano recital

DAY 5

A root word is a word that has a prefix, a suffix, or both attached to it. Read each word. Write the root word and the prefix or suffix in the correct boxes. Some words may have both a prefix and a suffix.

	Prefix	Root Word	Suffix
19. misfortune			
20. remove			
21. painless			
22. unusual			
23. disappear			

Calf Stretch

Stretching is an important part of any exercise program. Stretching increases a person's range of motion and can prevent muscle injury. Remember to warm up before stretching by walking around the block or jogging in place for several minutes.

One important stretch for many athletes is the calf stretch. Your calf muscle extends from your heel to the back of your knee. Stand facing a wall. Raise both arms in front of you with the palms of your hands flat against the wall. Press against the wall. Position your right leg behind you, heel flat on the ground. Your left leg should be bent and slightly in front of your right leg, closer to the wall. You should feel the stretch along the lower back of your right leg. Hold the stretch for 30 seconds. Switch sides.

CHARACTER CHECK: Think of someone you know who is courageous. Write a haiku poem about that person and share it with a family member.

* See page ii.

Find the least common multiple (LCM) for each set of numbers.

1.   6
     2
     LCM:

2.   4
     8
     LCM:

3.   5
     3
     LCM:

4.   4
     6
     LCM:

5.   8
     12
     LCM:

6.   6
     10
     LCM:

7.   6
     5
     15
     LCM:

8.   4
     9
     18
     LCM:

9.   4
     7
     14
     LCM:

Read each sentence. Circle the complete subject. Underline the complete predicate.

10.   The robin is considered to be a sign of spring in the Midwest.

11.   The Henderson family moved into an apartment on the 14th floor.

12.   I read about the extra traffic that creates problems during the winter.

13.   The US Open is a prestigious tennis tournament.

14.   Each member of the team deserves a trophy for his participation and hard work.

15.   Some rivers flow in a northern direction.

16.   Chang's family went hiking in Yellowstone National Park.

17.   Kelsey adopted the tiny, gray kitten from the animal shelter.

18.   Nora, Quinn, and Scott are going to the pool this afternoon.

DAY 6

Read the passage. Then, answer the questions.

The Great Wall of China

Stretching for more than 4,000 miles (6,400 km), the Great Wall of China is the longest structure ever built, and it was constructed entirely by hand. The wall is built from a variety of materials. Portions of the wall are assembled from crudely fashioned bricks. Some sections are made of stones. In the east, the wall has a foundation of granite blocks and sides of stone or brick. Where stone was scarce, workers used hardened earth, sand, or mud. In some areas, no mortar was used to hold the stones together.

The wall varies in height and width. Towers, which served as lookout stations, line many parts of the wall. Some sections of the wall were double layered to provide even more protection.

The Great Wall served as more than just protection from attacks. It also provided a physical boundary between China and northern lands. Winding its way through mountainous regions and bordering some desert areas, the wall was a well-fortified highway for traveling merchants.

The Great Wall has been **renovated** many times throughout the ages. Although parts of the wall have disappeared, some sections are in remarkably good condition. Now, steps are being taken to protect the wall from further destruction and deterioration.

19. Which of the following best defines the word *renovated*?
    A. relocated   B. revisited
    C. repaired   D. returned

20. Which of the following statements is false?
    A. Some sections of the wall were double layered for protection.
    B. Various sections of the wall were built from different materials.
    C. The wall is the longest structure ever built.
    D. The sections of the wall are all the same height and width.

21. How long is the Great Wall of China? _____

22. What did the Great Wall of China provide? _____

_____

_____

FACTOID: A polar bear's thick fur is actually clear, not white.

Rewrite each pair of fractions using the least common denominator (LCD).

1. $\frac{1}{9}$ and $\frac{1}{3}$ 2. $\frac{1}{3}$ and $\frac{1}{6}$ 3. $\frac{5}{6}$ and $\frac{2}{5}$

4. $\frac{3}{8}$ and $\frac{2}{3}$ 5. $\frac{1}{3}$ and $\frac{4}{9}$ 6. $\frac{4}{5}$ and $\frac{5}{9}$

7. $\frac{2}{4}$ and $\frac{3}{7}$ 8. $\frac{2}{3}$ and $\frac{7}{8}$ 9. $\frac{3}{5}$ and $\frac{5}{6}$

Underline the subject in each sentence. Then, circle the correct form of the verb.

10. Some of the beads (is, are) missing from the necklace.

11. Where (is, are) the gate to her house?

12. Tucson (lies, lie) to the south of Phoenix, Arizona.

13. A statue of Andrew Jackson (stand, stands) in Jackson Square.

14. The Dodgers, Braves, and Cardinals (is, are) division leaders.

Brandon Golston

Complete each sentence with a verb that makes sense and agrees with the subject.

15. Brittany and Mel _____ their homework immediately after school.

16. If the sheep are in the meadow, the cows _____ in the barn.

17. Tourists _____ warmer climates in the winter.

18. Christie _____ much more slowly than Merilee.

19. The home team fans always _____ louder than the
    visiting team fans.

DAY 7

Read each word. Write the root word and the prefix or suffix in the correct boxes. Some words may have both a prefix and a suffix.

	Prefix	Root Word	Suffix
20. misspell			
21. disagree			
22. reappear			
23. hopeless			
24. unlike			

The puzzles below use letters and words as clues to represent an idea, a phrase, or a saying. The placement and size of the words may help convey a puzzle's meaning. Look at the puzzles. Write the phrase, saying, or idea that each clue represents.

25.

Funny   Funny

Words   Words

Words   Words

_____

26.

All world

_____

27.

thodeepught

_____

28.

PRO
MISE

_____

FITNESS FLASH: Touch your toes 10 times.

* See page ii.

Write >, <, or = to compare each pair of fractions.

1. $\dfrac{3}{6}$ ☐ $\dfrac{4}{8}$

2. $\dfrac{4}{5}$ ☐ $\dfrac{10}{15}$

3. $\dfrac{3}{5}$ ☐ $\dfrac{1}{2}$

4. $\dfrac{2}{3}$ ☐ $\dfrac{5}{8}$

5. $\dfrac{1}{3}$ ☐ $\dfrac{2}{5}$

6. $\dfrac{1}{8}$ ☐ $\dfrac{1}{16}$

Write each set of fractions in order from least to greatest.

7. $\dfrac{1}{3}$, $\dfrac{7}{12}$, $\dfrac{5}{6}$

8. $\dfrac{3}{4}$, $\dfrac{7}{8}$, $\dfrac{13}{16}$

9. $\dfrac{3}{4}$, $\dfrac{5}{7}$, $\dfrac{9}{14}$

Underline the subject in each sentence. Then, circle the verb that agrees with the subject.

10. Carlos and Ben (has been, have been) friends since they were eight years old.

11. Lindsey (play, plays) basketball on the courts at her apartment building.

12. Both Anton and Holly (call, calls) New York City their home.

13. Trail Ridge Road (winds, wind) its way through Rocky Mountain National Park.

14. The questions on the test (was, were) easy to answer after studying so hard.

15. Kori (brings, bring) her iguana to school every year for "Pets on Parade Week."

16. The desk (look, looks) like an antique, but it is really a reproduction.

17. Riley and Duncan both (has, have) dogs for pets.

18. Kelsey (run, runs) every morning with her father.

DAY 8

Many foreign words and phrases are now commonly used in English speech. Read each sentence. Write the meaning of the italicized word or phrase on the line. Use a dictionary if you need help.

19. At the party, Dale spilled fruit punch on the carpet and was embarrassed by his *faux pas.* _____

20. Because there is little traffic there, Janice rides her bike around the *cul-de-sac* in her neighborhood. _____

21. In order to apply for a job as senior editor, Sam submitted his *résumé* to the human resources department. _____

22. My music teacher insists that my *forte* is rhythm. _____

Write the letter of each type of scientist next to the description of what the scientist studies. Use a dictionary if you need help.

A. agronomists	B. anthropologists	C. botanists
D. ecologists	E. entomologists	F. geneticists
G. marine biologists	H. paleontologists	I. zoologists

23. _____ plant life

24. _____ living and nonliving things in ecosystems

25. _____ relationships of organisms through DNA

26. _____ farms, crops, and soil

27. _____ animals and their classifications

28. _____ insects

29. _____ fossils and life forms of the past

30. _____ past and present-day human beings

31. _____ aquatic animals and plants

FACTOID: Every day, the human body replaces millions of worn-out cells.

Write each improper fraction as a whole number or a mixed number. Simplify if possible.

1. $\dfrac{4}{3} =$

2. $\dfrac{5}{2} =$

3. $\dfrac{25}{5} =$

4. $\dfrac{17}{12} =$

5. $\dfrac{10}{3} =$

6. $\dfrac{81}{9} =$

7. $\dfrac{43}{13} =$

8. $\dfrac{31}{5} =$

Write each mixed number as a simplified improper fraction.

9. $8\dfrac{2}{3} =$

10. $5\dfrac{2}{5} =$

11. $2\dfrac{9}{18} =$

12. $4\dfrac{3}{8} =$

13. $6\dfrac{3}{4} =$

14. $3\dfrac{3}{37} =$

15. $10\dfrac{2}{3} =$

16. $12\dfrac{3}{4} =$

Correct the paragraph. Look for errors in subject/verb agreement.

Monday Math Challenge

Every Monday, students in Mrs. Verdan's class works in pairs to complete math challenges. Each pair select its own working space. Gregory and Lea likes the table by the window. Lily and Masandra takes the round table near the door. Mandy and Zoe grabs the soft seats in the library corner. Each pair has 45 minutes to solve the puzzle. Most of them finishes on time. They shares their solutions with the whole class. Mrs. Verdan explain the solution and answer questions. Mrs. Verdan's students enjoys the weekly math challenges.

DAY 9

Read the passage. Then, answer the questions.

Hammurabi's Code

One reason that modern countries run smoothly is that their laws are published. Because of this, all citizens know the laws that they must follow. During ancient times, laws were not always recorded. A Babylonian king named Hammurabi created the first set of written laws for his people around 1760 BC. He wanted to bring all of the people in his empire together under one set of laws. Because the laws were written, everyone, whether rich or poor, was expected to obey them.

Hammurabi's Code included 282 laws written in cuneiform, a type of writing in which symbols were carved into clay tablets. Each law included a penalty, or punishment, for disobeying it. The laws were written on a **stela**, which was a large slab of stone posted for all to see. Archaeologists working in the area now known as Iran discovered the stela in 1901. Hammurabi's Code is now displayed in the Louvre Museum in Paris, France.

17. What is the main idea of this passage?
     A. Modern countries publish their laws.
     B. Hammurabi's Code is an ancient set of written laws.
     C. Archaeologists often find ancient materials.

18. Who was Hammurabi? _____

     _____

19. Why did Hammurabi write his laws? _____

     _____

     _____

     _____

20. What is a *stela*? _____

     _____

21. Where did archaeologists find Hammurabi's Code? _____

     _____

FITNESS FLASH: Do arm circles for 30 seconds.

* See page ii.

Solve each problem. Simplify if possible.

1. $\dfrac{5}{7} - \dfrac{4}{7} =$

2. $\dfrac{3}{10} + \dfrac{7}{10} =$

3. $\dfrac{7}{12} - \dfrac{1}{12} =$

4. $\dfrac{5}{6} + \dfrac{5}{6} =$

5. $\dfrac{2}{15} + \dfrac{8}{15} =$

6. $\dfrac{2}{5} + \dfrac{4}{5} =$

7. $\dfrac{15}{20} - \dfrac{8}{20} =$

8. $\dfrac{10}{11} - \dfrac{4}{11} =$

9. $\dfrac{9}{10} - \dfrac{4}{10} =$

10. $\dfrac{4}{9} + \dfrac{8}{9} =$

11. $\dfrac{3}{5} + \dfrac{4}{5} =$

12. $\dfrac{5}{6} + \dfrac{1}{6} =$

Underline the nouns in each sentence. Then, write each noun in the correct category.

13. Norman vacations on a peninsula in Maine.

14. The crowd clapped and cheered.

15. Carma studied the pollen of flowers.

16. Those mittens belong to Melanie.

17. The rabbit left tracks in the snow in our yard.

18. The cafeteria in our school is great.

People: _____

_____

Places: _____

_____

Things: _____

_____

DAY 10

An anagram is a word that is made by rearranging the letters of another word. Write the anagrams that best fit each pair of clues.

19. a type of cup _____

    candy that is chewed repeatedly _____

20. item worn by babies _____

    got back money that was loaned _____

21. a circle _____

    a place to swim that some people have in their yards _____

22. the rising and falling of the ocean level _____

    to correct a piece of writing _____

23. to move smoothly _____

    a hunting animal that lives in a pack _____

Respect **means treating people with courtesy and consideration. Think about a time when you saw a person show respect. Where were you? How did the person demonstrate respect? Choose one of the following situations. On another sheet of paper, draw a four-panel comic strip showing possible outcomes of people being respectful and disrespectful.**

A. It is the last week of school before summer vacation. You and your best friends are talking after lunch and enjoying being outdoors. Then, you hear the bell ring. Everyone walks toward the school and arrives at the entrance at the same time.

B. You are in the school cafeteria eating lunch with your friends. Students are busy eating and talking, and the room is very noisy. Suddenly, you notice that the principal has entered the cafeteria and is ready to make an announcement.

CHARACTER CHECK: Make a list of three things you can do at home that demonstrate cooperation. Post the list so that family members can add to it.

Solve each problem. Simplify if possible.

1. $8\frac{1}{5}$
    $-\ 3\frac{4}{5}$

2. $6\frac{1}{8}$
    $-\ 1\frac{2}{8}$

3. $9\frac{1}{9}$
    $-\ 3\frac{6}{9}$

4. $5\frac{2}{5}$
    $-\ 2\frac{3}{5}$

5. $4\frac{2}{8}$
    $-\ 3\frac{6}{8}$

6. $7\frac{2}{4}$
    $-\ 4\frac{3}{4}$

A common noun names a general person, place, thing, or idea. A proper noun names a specific person, place, thing, or idea. Circle the common nouns in each sentence. Underline the proper nouns.

7. The paint on the old barn is peeling.

8. A row of ants marched across the picnic blanket.

9. My mom loves to visit the beaches near Charleston, South Carolina.

10. Walter put on his boots before going outside.

11. Do alligators live in swamps?

12. Oliver wants to visit Paris, France.

13. Samantha borrowed three books from the library.

14. Jawan likes to eat at a restaurant called Good Eating.

15. . Is Ross going to the store with Jamie?

16. The dance will take place in the school gym.

DAY 11

Portmanteau words are made by combining two words. For example, *brunch* is a combination of the words *breakfast* and *lunch*. Combine each pair of words to make a portmanteau word.

17. flame + glare = _____

18. smoke + fog = _____

19. crispy + munch = _____

20. motor + hotel = _____

21. gleam + shimmer = _____

Label each map feature with a word from the word bank.

compass rose	legend	scale	title

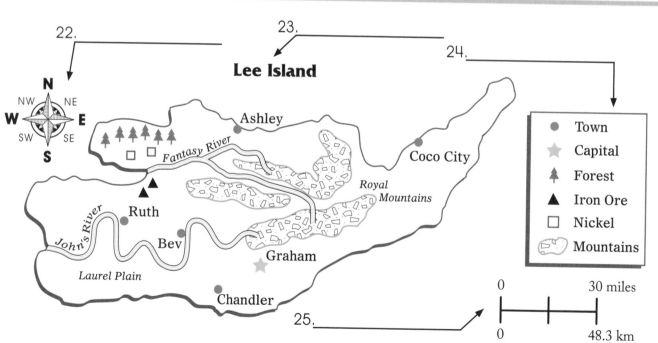

FACTOID: The Peregrine falcon can fly at speeds up to 186 miles (300 km) per hour.

Solve each problem. Simplify if possible.

1. $\frac{2}{3}$
    $+ \frac{1}{4}$

2. $\frac{5}{6}$
    $- \frac{4}{9}$

3. $\frac{2}{5}$
    $+ \frac{7}{10}$

4. $\frac{3}{8}$
    $- \frac{1}{4}$

5. $\frac{2}{3}$
    $- \frac{4}{9}$

6. $\frac{3}{8}$
    $+ \frac{5}{6}$

7. $\frac{1}{2}$
    $+ \frac{7}{8}$

8. $\frac{2}{3}$
    $- \frac{3}{5}$

9. $\frac{3}{10}$
    $+ \frac{3}{4}$

10. $\frac{5}{6}$
    $- \frac{1}{7}$

A concrete noun is a person, a place, or a thing. An abstract noun is an idea, an emotion, or a concept. Write **C** if the word is a concrete noun. Write **A** if the word is an abstract noun.

11. _____ joy

12. _____ bravery

13. _____ hair

14. _____ imagination

15. _____ peach

16. _____ freedom

17. _____ phone

18. _____ guitar

Is the noun *pride* a concrete noun or an abstract noun? Explain your decision.

_____

_____

_____

_____

_____

_____

DAY 12

Read each sentence. Then, circle the letter next to the correct meaning of the boldfaced word.

19. The engineers were afraid that the bridge would **buckle** under too much weight.
    A. piece of metal worn in the middle of a belt
    B. collapse or give way under pressure

20. The committee will **deliberate** on the issues.
    A. discuss before making a decision
    B. done on purpose after careful consideration

21. Please **relay** my message to the principal.
    A. communicate or pass along to
    B. race with a team of runners

22. We **scoured** the park for clues to the mystery.
    A. scrubbed clean
    B. searched thoroughly

23. A **plume** of smoke rose from the chimney.
    A. feather of a bird
    B. long column or band

If you could choose, would you rather be able to fly or to become invisible? Why? What other superpower would you like to have? Use another sheet of paper if you need more space.

_____

_____

_____

_____

 FITNESS FLASH: Practice a V-sit. Stretch five times.

* See page ii.

Solve each problem. Simplify if possible.

1. $6\frac{1}{4}$
   $-\ 4\frac{7}{16}$

2. $7\frac{1}{7}$
   $-\ 3\frac{6}{14}$

3. $8\frac{1}{3}$
   $-\ 2\frac{9}{15}$

4. $8\frac{1}{4}$
   $-\ 4\frac{6}{8}$

5. $9\frac{1}{18}$
   $-\ 5\frac{3}{6}$

6. $3\frac{1}{10}$
   $-\ 1\frac{4}{5}$

7. $5\frac{1}{16}$
   $-\ 4\frac{6}{8}$

8. $9\frac{2}{5}$
   $-\ 5\frac{3}{4}$

Write the plural form of each singular noun.

9. crash _____

10. tortilla _____

11. comic _____

12. melody _____

13. lady _____

14. gorilla _____

15. dentist _____

16. brush _____

17. address _____

18. berry _____

19. branch _____

20. zebra _____

21. glimpse _____

22. princess _____

23. responsibility _____

24. flamingo _____

25. business _____

26. climate _____

27. tax _____

28. bus _____

DAY 13

Read the movie schedule. Then, answer the questions.

Summer Movies
Afternoon and Evening Schedule

Cinema 6	Movie Mania	Theater Town
Oceans Apart 12:30 2:15 4:30	*Your Lucky Day* 12:30 2:15 4:30 7:00	*Feline Friends* 1:00 3:30 5:00
Land of Treasure 12:15 2:30 5:00	*Land of Treasure* 12:15 2:45 5:30 7:30	*Gridiron Greats* 1:00 3:15 5:30
Gridiron Greats 1:00 3:00 5:30	*Gridiron Greats* 1:30 4:00	*Time and Time Again* 12:30 3:45 6:15
Super Safari 1:00 3:30 6:00	*Super Safari* 2:30 5:30	*Your Lucky Day* 12:15 3:00 5:00
Your Lucky Day 12:00 3:30	*Oceans Apart* 3:00 6:00	*The Prairie Pals* 2:00 5:15
The Prairie Pals 12:00 3:30 6:15	*Feline Friends* 12:15 2:45 5:00	*Land of Treasure* 12:00 3:45 6:30

29. Which movie is scheduled for the latest show time at any of the theaters?

_____

30. It is 12:15 P.M. Valerie has a scout meeting at 4:00 P.M. Her family would like to see a movie before the meeting. Which of the following movies would fit their schedule, if each movie is two hours long?

    A. *Oceans Apart* at Movie Mania   B. *Gridiron Greats* at Theater Town

    C. *Your Lucky Day* at Cinema 6   D. *Super Safari* at Movie Mania

31. There are three children in the Sanchez family. Each child wants to see a different movie. Which theater is showing three different movies with the same starting time? _____

FACTOID: Africa's Sahara Desert is the size of the United States.

Day 16

1. 3%
2. 12%
3. 12.80%
4. 64.8%
5. 48%
6. 81%
7. 54.4%
8. 38.44%
9. 16%
10. 6%
11.
12. 190.07
13. for
14. about
15. on
16. into
17. to
18. beyond
19. after
20. in
21. to
22. into

23. Biographies & Mysteries
24. Similar   different
    n books.   bios - nonfiction
                       Mysteries - fiction

25. D.
26. B.
27. A
28. C
29. E
30. E

Mom   Dad   Dad Mom   Daug. Mom
Son   Daug.   Son Daug.   Son Dad

Daug, Son
Mom, Dad

Solve each problem. Show your work.

Mrs. Carlyle bought a bag of peanuts for her children. When Phillip, Joy, Brent, and Preston came home from school, they each took some peanuts from the bag.

- Phillip took $\frac{1}{3}$ of the peanuts from the bag.

- Joy took $\frac{1}{4}$ of the remaining peanuts.

- Brent took $\frac{1}{2}$ of the remaining peanuts.

- Preston took 10 peanuts.

- There were 71 peanuts remaining in the bag.

1. How many peanuts were originally in the bag? _____

2. How many peanuts did each child take? _____

_____

Draw a line through each incorrect plural. Then, write the correct irregular plural above it.

The Sheepdog Trial

Last autumn, our class went to a sheepdog trial. In this event, herding dogs competed

to move sheeps around fields and into enclosed areas. Two teachers, along with their

wifes and childs, came with us. It was autumn; the leafs were red and gold. We saw

oxes and wild gooses. The trial was held on a ranch. Before the trial, we watched

several mouses scurrying by the barn. At the beginning of each event, the sheeps

were released into a field. The dogs dashed out to herd them into an enclosure. All of

us jumped to our feets to applaud the dogs' skills.

Read each sentence. Then, circle the letter next to the correct meaning of the boldfaced word.

3. Deanna's **rash** decision caused her to lose the game.
    A. hasty or reckless
    B. skin inflammation

4. Mom paid a **toll** when we crossed the bridge.
    A. ring like a bell
    B. small tax or fee

5. Her **initial** reaction to the rain was to cancel the race.
    A. first or beginning
    B. the first letter of a person's name

6. The river has a very high **bank**.
    A. a place to keep money
    B. a slope or hill

7. We asked the cashier to **void** our transaction.
    A. cancel
    B. empty space

How would your life change without electricity and machines like cars? Describe the things in your life that would change and the things that would stay the same. Would life be better or worse? Why? Use another sheet of paper if you need more space.

_____

_____

_____

_____

_____

FITNESS FLASH: Do arm circles for 30 seconds.

* See page ii.

Solve each problem. Simplify if possible.

1. $\dfrac{3}{7} \times \dfrac{4}{5} =$

2. $\dfrac{4}{5} \times \dfrac{6}{8} =$

3. $\dfrac{2}{3} \times \dfrac{4}{7} =$

4. $\dfrac{5}{6} \times \dfrac{4}{5} =$

5. $\dfrac{2}{3} \times \dfrac{7}{8} =$

6. $\dfrac{7}{9} \times \dfrac{8}{9} =$

7. $\dfrac{1}{2} \times \dfrac{2}{12} =$

8. $\dfrac{2}{3} \times \dfrac{4}{12} =$

9. $\dfrac{6}{8} \times \dfrac{4}{16} =$

An antecedent is the word or phrase to which a pronoun refers. Underline the antecedent in each sentence. Then, circle the pronoun that agrees in number with the antecedent.

10. Our neighbor brought (her, their) dog to play at our house.

11. Since it has been getting cold, I told the guests to bring (his, their, your) coats.

12. The lawyer often collaborates with (our, her, their) colleagues.

13. Students who complete all of (his, her, their) homework assignments often do well on tests.

14. If anyone else wants to go on the field trip, (he, it, they) should bring a note from home tomorrow.

15. The girl needs to have (her, she, their) own art supplies for class.

16. The council members voiced (his, her, their) opinions at the town hall meeting.

17. One of the boys on the bus gave (her, his, our) seat to the woman.

18. Michelle and Alicia made (her, they, their) mother breakfast.

Read each sentence. Then, circle the letter next to the correct meaning of the boldfaced word.

19. To what **degree** do you agree with his remarks?
    A. measurement of temperature
    B. extent of a condition

20. The tapestry has **elaborate** designs on it.
    A. detailed or complex
    B. tell more about

21. The map has a **legend** to tell us what the symbols mean.
    A. story told from the past
    B. explanation of symbols

22. The bike shop charges a **flat** rate for replacing tires.
    A. set or not varying
    B. smooth and even

23. Mom said that my new glasses **suit** me.
    A. look appropriate on
    B. matched set of clothing

Dance Fever!

Show off your ability to dance to different musical tempos. Choose songs that have different speeds and have a friend or adult play small parts of each song. Start dancing and adjust your speed to each song's tempo. Stretch all of your major muscle groups with movements such as bending forward, arching your back, and lifting your arms above your head. Remember to warm up and cool down with a slow song and stretch slowly at first.

> **CHARACTER CHECK:** Make a list of three things you can do at home that demonstrate cooperation. Share your list with a family member.

* See page ii.

Solve each problem. Write each improper fraction as a simplified mixed number.

1. $\dfrac{1}{15} \times 5 =$

2. $\dfrac{5}{14} \times 7 =$

3. $\dfrac{1}{16} \times 8 =$

4. $\dfrac{6}{15} \times 4 =$

5. $\dfrac{5}{12} \times 6 =$

6. $\dfrac{3}{16} \times 8 =$

7. $3 \times \dfrac{4}{15} =$

8. $5 \times \dfrac{10}{12} =$

9. $5 \times \dfrac{3}{6} =$

Circle the pronoun or pronouns that correctly complete each sentence.

10. Sara and Bonnie took (they, them) to the matinee.

11. After the snowstorm, (us, we) helped shovel the walkway.

12. Cameron helped (she, her) find the lens from (her, hers) glasses.

13. (I, Me) planted many seeds in (our, ours) garden.

14. Will (you, your) come with (I, me) to (their, theirs) house?

15. Joe loaned (he, his) new baseball glove to (she, her).

16. Did (her, she) blame (we, us) for the broken window?

17. Tye will help Justin and (I, me) look for (it, its).

18. (We, Us) can build (it, its) over there in (your, yours) big tree.

19. Owen and (I, me) took an art course this summer.

DAY 16

Read the passage. Then, answer the questions.

Fossils

Fossils are the remains of plants or animals from thousands of years ago that have turned to stone. After the organisms died, their bodies were buried in sediment and gradually replaced by minerals. Sometimes, an animal's bones, teeth, or shell are preserved. Other times, only an impression of its body is made. Footprints, eggs, and nests can also be fossilized.

Fossils can be found in many places. They are frequently uncovered when people dig up the earth as they build roads. Also, fossils often are buried in layers of rock and are exposed through erosion of a mountainside. Others are found during undersea excavation. Scientists study fossils to learn what the living animals and plants looked like. They can use radiocarbon dating to find out how old a fossil is. All living things contain carbon, so scientists measure how much carbon is left in a fossil to determine its age.

20. What is the main idea of this passage?

   A.   Radiocarbon dating helps scientists determine the age of fossils.

   B.   Sometimes, only an impression of a plant is left.

   C.   Fossils are plant or animal remains from long ago.

21. What happens when something is fossilized? _____

_____

22. What parts of an animal's body might be preserved? _____

_____

23. Why do scientists study fossils? _____

_____

24. How does radiocarbon dating help determine a fossil's age? _____

_____

_____

_____

FACTOID: There are approximately twice as many kangaroos in Australia as there are people.

Solve each problem. Write each improper fraction as a simplified mixed number.

1. $\dfrac{1}{3} \times 3\dfrac{1}{4} =$

2. $\dfrac{1}{2} \times 2\dfrac{1}{5} =$

3. $\dfrac{2}{4} \times 2\dfrac{1}{6} =$

4. $\dfrac{3}{6} \times 4\dfrac{3}{4} =$

5. $\dfrac{4}{8} \times 5\dfrac{2}{3} =$

6. $6\dfrac{1}{3} \times \dfrac{1}{8} =$

7. $2\dfrac{3}{4} \times \dfrac{3}{5} =$

8. $4\dfrac{2}{5} \times \dfrac{3}{4} =$

9. $1\dfrac{2}{7} \times \dfrac{2}{4} =$

Circle each possessive pronoun. Draw an arrow to the noun that it modifies.

10. Their mom travels around the state on business.

11. Our house is near the library.

12. Its handle is loose.

13. The black dog beside the tree is mine.

14. Her socks are in the middle drawer.

15. We went to the musical with his parents.

16. The house with the pool is his.

17. My friend asked my opinion about which bike to buy.

18. The vegetable and cream cheese sandwich is hers.

19. Their wooded backyard is a great place to play.

DAY 17

The emotion associated with a word is its connotation. Read each word. Write *P* if the word has a positive connotation. Write *N* if the word has a negative connotation. Then, find each word in a dictionary and write its denotation.

20. _____ desolate _____

21. _____ serene _____

22. _____ noble _____

23. _____ betray _____

24. _____ intrepid _____

Unscramble each word to form the name of an Eastern or Western European country. Use a map if you need help.

25. diarnel _____

26. saursi _____

27. ngeyram _____

28. atruisa _____

29. kndaemr _____

30. ktuery _____

31. dsewne _____

32. tlaiva _____

33. apgrotlu _____

34. rsuelba _____

 FITNESS FLASH: Practice a V-sit. Stretch five times.

* See page ii.

Solve each problem. Write each improper fraction as a simplified mixed number.

1. $3\frac{1}{3} \times 4\frac{1}{4} =$

2. $2\frac{1}{5} \times 1\frac{1}{6} =$

3. $2\frac{1}{4} \times 2\frac{1}{2} =$

4. $1\frac{1}{6} \times 2\frac{1}{7} =$

5. $4\frac{1}{8} \times 1\frac{1}{8} =$

6. $3\frac{1}{2} \times 3\frac{3}{4} =$

7. $1\frac{1}{4} \times 3\frac{2}{5} =$

8. $2\frac{1}{3} \times 1\frac{6}{8} =$

9. $2\frac{4}{5} \times 3\frac{1}{6} =$

Circle the indefinite pronouns in each sentence.

10. Many will come to the museum this summer.

11. A hummingbird came to the feeder this morning, and others came last night.

12. Someone got the crowd to cheer excitedly.

13. Only a few registered, but several arrived on the day of the race.

14. I think somebody should clean up the marbles and game pieces.

15. Walter and Mason are here with a mower; either can mow the yard.

16. Anybody who gets home before me can put dinner in the oven.

17. Fruits and vegetables are delicious; each is good for a healthy, growing body.

18. Jessie liked the sweaters and wanted to buy both.

19. Some have blue tags, and others have red tags.

DAY 18

Read each pair of words. Write **P** next to the word with a positive connotation. Write **N** next to the word with a negative connotation. Then, look up each word in a dictionary and write its denotation.

20. _____ thrifty _____

_____ cheap _____

21. _____ picky _____

_____ selective _____

22. _____ pushy _____

_____ assertive _____

23. _____ haughty _____

_____ proud _____

How are animal cells and plant cells alike? How are they different? For each cell characteristic below, write *plant*, *animal*, or *both* on the line.

24. _____ These cells have cell membranes.

25. _____ These cells use chloroplasts for photosynthesis.

26. _____ These cells use mitosis to divide into two daughter cells.

27. _____ Each of these cells has one or more large vacuoles.

28. _____ Instead of a few large vacuoles, these cells have several small vacuoles.

29. _____ These cells have cell walls that usually give the cells a rectangular shape.

30. _____ Each of these cells has a nucleus that controls all of the cell's functions.

31. _____ These cells have irregular shapes.

32. _____ Mitochondria help create energy for these cells.

FACTOID: An adult elephant can eat 550 pounds (249.5 kg) of vegetation each day.

Fractions/Parts of Speech

Solve each problem. Write each improper fraction as a simplified mixed number.

1. $6 \times 2\frac{1}{3} =$
2. $7 \times 2\frac{1}{5} =$
3. $3 \times 2\frac{1}{5} =$

4. $2 \times 1\frac{3}{8} =$
5. $5 \times 4\frac{2}{4} =$
6. $6 \times 2\frac{4}{5} =$

7. $2\frac{1}{3} \times 3 =$
8. $1\frac{1}{8} \times 5 =$
9. $1\frac{1}{4} \times 6 =$

A reflexive pronoun indicates that a person or thing is both initiating and receiving the action of a sentence. Underline the reflexive pronoun in each sentence.

10. The woman in Leonardo da Vinci's painting, the *Mona Lisa*, seems to be smiling to herself.

11. For centuries, people have asked themselves why this is so.

12. I have wondered myself about her mysterious smile.

13. Leonardo da Vinci kept that secret to himself.

14. If you want to see the *Mona Lisa* for yourself, go to the Louvre Museum in Paris, France.

Complete each sentence with the correct reflexive pronoun in parentheses.

15. Leonardo developed a new painting technique by _____. (itself, himself)

16. The wall _____ was Leonardo's canvas. (himself, itself)

17. I have tried the technique _____ and found it challenging. (myself, ourselves)

DAY 19

Read the passage. Then, answer the questions.

The Great Barrier Reef

The Great Barrier Reef is considered by many people to be one of the seven natural wonders of the world. The reef stretches for more than 1,200 miles (1,931 km) off the coast of northeast Australia. It is the largest coral structure in the world, the largest structure ever constructed by living organisms, and the only living thing on Earth that is visible from outer space.

The Great Barrier Reef consists mostly of coral, a rocklike substance made by tiny animals. These tiny animals, called polyps, are too numerous to count. The polyps are born in a continuous cycle of reproducing, eating, and dying. New coral is slowly added to the reef through this process.

The **fragile** reef is continually changing its shape and color. These changes are caused by many factors, including the polyps' constant activities. People visiting the reef and changes in the environment can damage the reef through pollution or carelessness. Harmful animals, such as the crown of thorns starfish, can also destroy the reef, especially when environmental changes contribute to their overpopulation.

18. The tiny animals that make the Great Barrier Reef are called _____ .

19. Where is the Great Barrier Reef located? _____

_____

20. Circle the letter next to each statement that is true.
    A. The Great Barrier Reef has not changed for centuries.
    B. The Great Barrier Reef stretches for more than 1,200 miles (1,931 km).
    C. The Great Barrier Reef can be seen from outer space.
    D. The Great Barrier Reef is the second largest coral structure in the world.

21. What does the word *fragile* mean?_____

22. Write three factors that cause the reef to change. _____

_____

_____

FITNESS FLASH: Do 10 shoulder shrugs.

* See page ii.

Solve each problem.

1. $\frac{2}{5}$ of 10

2. $\frac{5}{6}$ of 24

3. $\frac{4}{5}$ of 60

4. $\frac{3}{4}$ of 44

5. $\frac{7}{10}$ of 80

6. $\frac{6}{25}$ of 125

7. $\frac{5}{8}$ of 96

8. $\frac{7}{12}$ of 144

9. Four-sevenths of the students in Mrs. Mason's sixth-grade class are girls. If there are 28 students in Mrs. Mason's class, how many of them are girls?

10. Three-fifths of the cookies on the tray are chocolate chip. If there are 120 cookies on the tray, how many cookies are chocolate chip?

Draw a line through each incorrectly used pronoun. Write the correct pronoun above it.

Art Club Memo

Dear Craft Club Members,

Whomever forgot to return the scissors should bring it back to the art room. A few pairs were missing from the room after our meeting. In the future, someone will be allowed to remove supplies from the room. The school trusts us, and we have a responsibility to leave the workspace as we found them. I am sure that these was a mistake. That is why I am asking each member to check he backpack. Call me if you find they. Thank you for you help!

Sincerely,

Liz

DAY 20

Look at each word. Make a new word by leaving out one letter and keeping the remaining letters in the same order. Continue until a two-letter word remains.

11. splint

_____

_____

_____

_____

12. pounce

_____

_____

_____

_____

13. friend

_____

_____

_____

_____

14. paints

_____

_____

_____

_____

When you go to a fair or an amusement park, do you prefer to ride the rides, play games, eat food, or watch people? Why is that activity your favorite? Use another sheet of paper if you need more space.

_____

_____

_____

_____

_____

_____

_____

_____

CHARACTER CHECK: Throughout the day, look for people who are encouraging others. At the end of the day, talk with a family member about the encouragement you observed.

The Heart of the Matter

How does exercise affect your heart rate?

Each time the ventricles of your heart contract, blood is forced into your arteries. Each heartbeat makes your arteries stretch, which causes the pulsing sensation that you feel. As blood is being pushed out of your heart, it moves very quickly so that it can reach parts of your body that are far from your heart.

Materials:

- watch with a second hand

Procedure:

Sit on the floor or in a chair and relax for one minute. Use your index and middle fingers to locate your pulse in either your wrist or neck. Count the number of times that you feel your heart beat for 15 seconds. Multiply this number by four. This will be your resting pulse rate for one minute. Record this number on the chart below.

Jog in place for one minute. Then, stop jogging and use your index and middle fingers to locate your pulse in your wrist or neck. Count the number of times that you feel your heart beat for 15 seconds. Multiply this number by four. Record this number in the "Active Heart Rate" column. Repeat these steps two additional times. Then, calculate your average resting and active heart rates by adding the three trials and dividing by three. Finally, answer the question below.

Results:

Trial	Resting Heart Rate	Active Heart Rate
1		
2		
3		
Average:		

How did exercise affect your heart rate? _____

_____

BONUS

Newton's First Law

Will an object at rest stay at rest and an object in motion stay in motion unless acted upon by another force? In this activity, you will test Newton's first law.

Materials:
- plastic cup
- coin
- index card

Procedure:

Cover the top of the cup with the index card. Put the coin on top of the card. Think about how you can get the coin inside of the cup without touching the coin or lifting or tilting the index card.

Test your ideas and see if you can get the coin into the cup. After you have gotten the coin into the cup, answer each question.

1. How did you get the coin into the cup? _____

_____

_____

2. What happens to the coin if the card is moved away slowly?

_____

_____

3. Why does the coin drop into the cup? _____

_____

_____

_____

4. Can you think of a place where you have seen something similar happen?

_____

_____

_____

Latitude and Longitude

Write the name of the North American city that is found at each latitude and longitude reading.

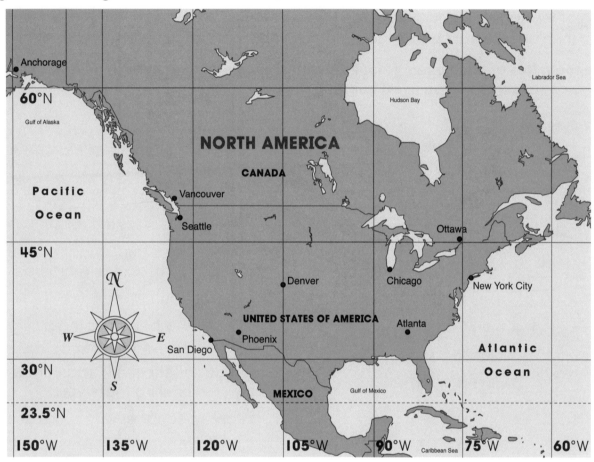

1. 61°13'N, 149°54'W

2. 33°45'N, 84°23'W

3. 41°50'N, 87°37'W

4. 39°45'N, 105°W

5. 47°37'N, 122°20'W

6. 33°29'N, 112°4'W

7. 32°42'N, 117°10'W

8. 40°47'N, 73°58'W

9. 45°24'N, 75°43'W

10. 49°13'N, 123°06'W

BONUS

Roman Time Line

Latium, on the west coast of Italy, was the site of a group of villages near the Tiber River. Here, according to legend, Rome was founded in 753 BC by Romulus after he killed his twin brother, Remus. Romulus became Rome's first king. Kings ruled Rome until 510 BC. Rome then became a republic, governed by the Senate, a group of citizens.

Write the letter of each event from Roman history on the line next to its date. Use reference resources if you need help.

1. _____ 241 BC
2. _____ 218 BC
3. _____ 206 BC
4. _____ 146 BC
5. _____ 60 BC
6. _____ 44 BC
7. _____ 31 BC–AD 14
8. _____ AD 98–117
9. _____ AD 117–138
10. _____ AD 138–161
11. _____ AD 193
12. _____ AD 293
13. _____ AD 306–337
14. _____ AD 313

A. On March 15 (Ides of March), Julius Caesar is killed.
B. Trajan is emperor.
C. Hannibal crosses the Alps.
D. The throne is auctioned to Didius Julianus, who is later murdered.
E. The First Triumvirate rules.
F. Christianity becomes the official religion of Rome.
G. Augustus, the first Roman emperor, reigned during these years.
H. Rome occupies Sicily, Corsica, and Sardinia.
I. Antoninus Pius is emperor. Rome's power is at its peak.
J. Rome captures Spain.
K. Diocletian divides the empire into a tetrarchy.
L. Hadrian is emperor.
M. Carthage is destroyed.
N. Constantine reigns during these years and reunites the empire.

World Landmarks

Write the correct number to identify each world landmark. Then, complete the table by writing the country where each landmark is located. Use reference resources if you need help.

Number	Landmark	Country
1	Great Wall of China	
2	Statue of Liberty	
3	Great Sphinx	
4	Taj Mahal	
5	Colosseum	
6	Stonehenge	
7	Eiffel Tower	
8	Chichen Itza	

BONUS

Take It Outside!

Summer is a great time to explore your community. Brainstorm a list of five landmarks in your town, city, or county and identify these locations on a map. Then, invite your family and friends to join you on a landmark tour of your community. Bring a camera, a pen, and a notebook. At each landmark, take a group photo and ask each person for a comment about the landmark. After the tour, create a photo collage showing your friends and family at the landmarks along with their captioned comments.

With an adult, visit a local farmers' market. Bring a pen and a notebook and record the items that you observe for sale. Talk with the vendors about the things they are selling and the benefits of buying fresh produce. Once you are back home, review your notes and use them to create a 30-second commercial for the farmers' market. Record your commercial and share it with family, friends, and neighbors.

Go for a walk around your neighborhood with an adult. Take a pen and a notebook. Record the different types of animals that you see, using tally marks to indicate multiple viewings of one type of animal. After your walk, review your notes. Then, show the results of your animal observation walk by creating a bar graph. Which animal did you find to be most prevalent in your neighborhood?

Monthly Goals

Think of three goals to set for yourself this month. For example, you may want to read for 30 minutes each day. Write your goals on the lines. Post them someplace visible, where you will see them every day.

Place a check mark next to each goal that you complete. Feel proud that you have met your goals and set new ones to continue to challenge yourself.

1. _____
2. _____
3. _____

Word List

The following words are used in this section. Use a dictionary to look up each word that you do not know. Then, write three sentences. Use at least one word from the word list in each sentence.

architecture	incessant
biome	molecules
constellation	prospectors
dramatically	renaissance
hieroglyphics	tundra

1. _____
   _____
2. _____
   _____
3. _____
   _____

Introduction to Strength

This section includes fitness and character development activities that focus on strength. These activities are designed to get you moving and thinking about strengthening your body and your character.

Physical Strength

Like flexibility, strength is important for a healthy body. Many people think that a strong person is someone who can lift an enormous amount of weight. However, strength is more than the ability to pick up heavy barbells. Having strength is important for many everyday activities, such as helping with yardwork or lifting a younger sibling into a car seat. Muscular strength also helps reduce stress on your joints as your body ages.

Everyday activities and many fun exercises provide opportunities for you to build strength. Carrying bags of groceries, riding a bicycle, and swimming are all excellent ways to strengthen your muscles. Classic exercises, such as push-ups and chin-ups, are also fantastic strength builders.

Set realistic, achievable goals to improve your strength based on the activities you enjoy. Evaluate your progress during the summer months and, as you accomplish your strength goals, set new goals to challenge yourself.

Strength of Character

As you build your physical strength, work on your inner strength as well. Having a strong character means standing up for your beliefs, even if others do not agree with your viewpoint. Inner strength can be shown in many ways. For example, you can show inner strength by being honest, standing up for someone who needs your help, and putting your best effort into every task. It is not always easy to show inner strength. Think of a time when you showed inner strength, such as telling the truth when you broke your mother's favorite vase. How did you use your inner strength to handle that situation?

Use the summer months to develop a strong sense of self, both physically and emotionally. Celebrate your successes and look for ways to become even stronger. Reflect upon your accomplishments during the summer, and you will see positive growth on the inside as well as on the outside.

Solve the problem.

Sadie put a $20 bill into a change machine. The machine gave her two bills worth the same amount. Sadie put one of the bills in her pocket. She put the other bill back into the change machine. The change machine gave her two bills worth the same amount. Sadie kept one of those bills, and she put the other bill back into the change machine. The change machine gave her five bills worth the same amount.

1. How many bills does Sadie have now? _____

2. What is the amount of each bill? _____

_____

Underline the linking verb in each sentence.

3. The knitted mittens are very warm.

4. The food on the table appears fresh.

5. The neighbor's dog is a dalmatian.

6. The garbage can by the door is full.

7. Trey's homemade sorbet is delicious and refreshing.

8. The letters my mother sent to me become more special every year.

9. Haley, April's big sister, is our junior counselor.

10. Amber, my younger cousin, was in first grade last year.

11. The moon was like a huge orange ball hovering in the sky.

12. The music grew increasingly louder.

DAY 1

A simile is a comparison between two things that uses the words *like* or *as*.
Read each sentence. Underline the simile and draw an arrow to what or who it is
describing. Then, write what each simile means.

13. Mom did not feel well last week, but now she is as fit as a fiddle.

    _____

14. The detective had to be as smart as a fox to solve the mystery.

    _____

15. Her smile is like sunshine on a cloudy day.

    _____

16. His footsteps sounded like thunder on the wooden floor.

    _____

Study the words in the word bank and decide what the column headings should be.
Then, classify the animals listed in the word bank.

alligator	bear	crab	frog	goose
hawk	monkey	mosquito	owl	raven
snake	squirrel	tortoise	trout	whale

FACTOID: Ostriches can run as fast as 40 miles (64.4 km) per hour.

Write the reciprocal of each number or fraction.

1. $\dfrac{11}{5} \times \boxed{\dfrac{}{}} = 1$

2. $2\dfrac{1}{4} \times \boxed{\dfrac{}{}} = 1$

3. $9 \times \boxed{\dfrac{}{}} = 1$

4. $\dfrac{3}{10} \times \boxed{\dfrac{}{}} = 1$

5. $\dfrac{1}{7} \times \boxed{\dfrac{}{}} = 1$

6. $4\dfrac{5}{8} \times \boxed{\dfrac{}{}} = 1$

7. $\dfrac{15}{11} \times \boxed{\dfrac{}{}} = 1$

8. $\dfrac{1}{6} \times \boxed{\dfrac{}{}} = 1$

9. $\dfrac{3}{4} \times \boxed{\dfrac{}{}} = 1$

10. $3 \times \boxed{\dfrac{}{}} = 1$

11. $\dfrac{9}{4} \times \boxed{\dfrac{}{}} = 1$

12. $7\dfrac{5}{8} \times \boxed{\dfrac{}{}} = 1$

Underline the whole verb phrase in each sentence. Circle each helping verb.

13. The water is pouring into the basement.

14. The rabbit had scurried into the hole.

15. We are going to the amusement park.

16. The lights can be dimmed with this switch.

17. Max was taking his turn.

18. The puppy must have tried to jump onto the bed.

19. That jam would be good on toast.

20. The bird had flown into the bushes.

21. We should pull the weeds out of the garden.

22. Asya may have been going to the zoo.

DAY 2

Read the passage. Then, answer the questions.

The Renaissance

Renaissance is a French word that means *rebirth*. Between AD 1350 and AD 1600, Europeans experienced a rebirth in the arts, literature, and science. In the Middle Ages, people forgot many of the ancient Greeks' and Romans' achievements because their daily lives were so hard. During the Renaissance, people began to reread ancient texts and create new art, literature, and architecture. One Renaissance author was William Shakespeare. His plays are still performed today. Many important Renaissance artists lived in Italy, including Michelangelo, Raphael, and Titian. The most famous figure of this period might be Leonardo da Vinci, who excelled in the areas of art, architecture, and science. Da Vinci's sketchbooks contain drawings of helicopters and airplanes, hundreds of years before they were even invented. When someone is referred to as a "Renaissance man" or a "Renaissance woman," it means that the person is good at many different things, like Leonardo da Vinci.

23. What is the main idea of this passage?

    A. During the Renaissance, people created new art forms.

    B. Many people learned to paint during the Renaissance.

    C. The Renaissance was an important time for science, literature, and the arts.

24. How long did the Renaissance last? _____

25. What happened during the Renaissance? _____

_____

_____

26. How can you tell that Shakespeare was a great writer? _____

_____

_____

27. In which areas did Leonardo da Vinci excel? _____

_____

FITNESS FLASH: Do five push-ups.

Solve each problem. Write each improper fraction as a simplified mixed number.

1. $\dfrac{7}{2} \div \dfrac{1}{2} =$

2. $\dfrac{4}{3} \div \dfrac{2}{3} =$

3. $\dfrac{6}{4} \div \dfrac{3}{4} =$

4. $\dfrac{9}{2} \div \dfrac{1}{3} =$

5. $\dfrac{8}{3} \div \dfrac{2}{5} =$

6. $\dfrac{15}{4} \div \dfrac{3}{7} =$

7. $\dfrac{5}{6} \div \dfrac{5}{6} =$

8. $\dfrac{3}{8} \div \dfrac{3}{4} =$

9. $\dfrac{3}{4} \div \dfrac{5}{2} =$

The subject of a passive-voice sentence is acted upon. The subject of an active-voice sentence performs the action. Rewrite each sentence in the active voice.

10. Experiments have been conducted by students to test the hypothesis.

_____

11. The exam was passed by more than two-thirds of the applicants.

_____

12. The song is sung by the choir at every graduation.

_____

13. The vegetarian pizza was enjoyed by all of my friends.

_____

14. The nail was hammered into the wall by Cameron.

_____

DAY 3

A metaphor is a comparison between two things that does not use the words *like* or *as*. Read each sentence. Underline the two things that are being compared. Then, write what each metaphor means.

15.   That test was a piece of cake.

_____

16.   Winning the award was a dream come true.

_____

17.   Our backyard was a blanket of snow.

_____

18.   My pillow was a cloud after the long day.

_____

19.   The lake was a mirror surrounded by tall, old trees.

_____

Like animals, plants adapt to fit their environments. Match each method of adaptation to the name of a plant.

20.   _____   Its roots can absorb oxygen from water.   A.   desert cactus

21.   _____   Its slimy, juicy tissue stores water in the   B.   rosebush
                    dry season.

22.   _____   Its stems have thorns to keep predators   C.   fern
                    from eating its flowers.

23.   _____   It produces many spores, which are   D.   reed at a
                    dispersed by wind and water.   pond's edge

24.   _____   Its slim needles allow heavy snow to fall   E.   pine tree on a
                    through them.   tall mountain

FACTOID: An elephant seal can dive 5,000 feet (1.52 km) underwater while searching for food.

Solve each problem. Write each improper fraction as a simplified mixed number.

1. $6 \div \dfrac{4}{9} =$

2. $5 \div \dfrac{1}{7} =$

3. $\dfrac{4}{7} \div 8 =$

4. $4 \div \dfrac{3}{5} =$

5. $\dfrac{5}{8} \div 5 =$

6. $\dfrac{9}{10} \div 4 =$

7. $\dfrac{9}{4} \div 6 =$

8. $4 \div \dfrac{5}{3} =$

9. $\dfrac{4}{3} \div 5 =$

Draw a line through each incorrect verb. Then, write the correct verb above each crossed-out verb.

Game Day

Once a month, our school hold a game day in the gymnasium. We participate in races and other games. Fernando and Melvin always races on the same team. They enjoys running. Target toss is a favorite event. Each player toss the ball at a target painted on the wall. Laura and Jordana usually win because they practices after school. José and Luke like basketball. Kyle and Spencer usually scores more points, but José and Luke is improving all of the time. At the end of the day, teams from two classes play a game of volleyball.

DAY 4

Read each sentence and underline the idiom. Then, write what each idiom means.

10. Angela is always ready to help her friends at the drop of a hat.

_____

11. Mom says that my brother has an iron stomach.

_____

12. Our neighbors bent over backward to help us when we moved in next door.

_____

13. The store's manager said that they were selling everything but the kitchen sink.

_____

14. Janie was on pins and needles while she waited for the concert to begin.

_____

Wall Push-Ups

Strong muscles and bones are important for fitness and overall health. This exercise will help strengthen your arms, shoulders, and back. You will need three to four feet (0.9–1.2 m) of empty wall space and a few minutes each day, and soon you will reap the benefits of a stronger body.

This exercise is like doing a push-up against a wall instead of on the floor. To begin, stand straight and face the wall. Place your hands shoulder-width apart against the wall with your fingers pointing up. You should be standing far enough away from the wall that your elbows are only slightly bent.

As you inhale, bend your elbows and bring your face toward the wall. Exhale and push against the wall, straightening your arms until you have returned to the starting position. Remember to keep your body straight. Keep your heels as close to the floor as you can. Do two sets of 8–10 repetitions. For a challenge, try moving your hands farther apart or rotate your palms so that your fingers face slightly inward or outward.

FITNESS FLASH: Do 10 lunges.

* See page ii.

Solve each problem. Write each improper fraction as a simplified mixed number.

1. $11\frac{1}{2} \div 2\frac{7}{8} =$

2. $3\frac{1}{2} \div 2 =$

3. $4\frac{1}{4} \div 3\frac{1}{8} =$

4. $3\frac{3}{4} \div 5 =$

5. $3\frac{1}{2} \div 1\frac{3}{4} =$

6. $6\frac{1}{3} \div 2 =$

7. $8 \div 1\frac{1}{5} =$

8. $12\frac{3}{8} \div 2\frac{3}{4} =$

9. $5\frac{3}{5} \div 4\frac{2}{3} =$

A direct object is the noun or pronoun that receives the action of a verb and tells _who_ or _what_. Underline the verb in each sentence. Circle each direct object.

10. The courtyard fountain continuously gushed water.

11. Leona frequently chews gum.

12. The anxious horse kicked the stall door.

13. Erica handed Jacob her paper.

14. Rochelle stowed the luggage in the overhead bin.

15. Danielle offered her carrots to Jesse.

16. Rosa canceled her subscription to the magazine.

17. Yolanda crochets one blanket each month.

18. Debbie made vegetable soup for dinner.

19. Enrique toasted a marshmallow over the campfire.

Read the passage. Then, answer the questions.

Rachel Carson

After World War II, farmers began using pesticides, such as DDT, to protect their crops. Near the farmlands where the pesticides were used, birds and animals were dying. Scientist Rachel Carson felt that she had to do something. She wrote a book in 1962 titled *Silent Spring* that described forests that were quiet and land that was dying.

Carson loved the outdoors, and she studied wildlife and marine biology in school. She worked as a scientist for the government and also wrote about natural history. Soon, she was in charge of all of the writing done by the U.S. Fish and Wildlife Service.

In 1941, Carson published her first book, *Under the Sea-Wind*. She published her second book, *The Sea Around Us*, in 1951. In 1955, she published a third book, *The Edge of the Sea*. Carson described life on the seashore and the animals and plants that lived in the oceans. Her books became national best sellers.

Then, Carson learned that she was seriously ill with cancer. At the same time, she began reading reports about DDT. Carson feared that she did not have a lot of time left to help. She wanted to keep writing about the sea, but she felt that it was more important to keep **toxic** chemicals away from crops and animals.

Silent Spring's publication caused a storm of argument about chemicals. The chemical companies said that the book was inaccurate, but Carson was certain that DDT was toxic. She spoke before the U.S. Congress, asking for new laws to protect the environment. President John F. Kennedy formed a committee to study the issue, and the committee confirmed the results of Carson's research. Congress passed laws about the use of DDT and the testing of other chemicals.

Carson died two years later. But, her work is still remembered, and efforts to protect the living world from chemicals and other dangers continue.

20. What does the word *toxic* mean? _____

21. What made Rachel Carson stop writing about the sea? _____

_____

_____

22. What did Carson study in school? _____

> **CHARACTER CHECK:** Make a list of at least three ways you can show patience at home. Share the list with a family member.

Add or subtract to solve each problem.

1.
$$7.59$$
$$+ \ 2.09$$

2.
$$25.90$$
$$+ \ 34.80$$

3.
$$157.8$$
$$+ \ 30.1$$

4.
$$83.041$$
$$+ \ 5.226$$

5.
$$10.42$$
$$- \ 6.01$$

6.
$$52.99$$
$$- \ 25.00$$

7.
$$14.07$$
$$- \ 2.88$$

8.
$$19.99$$
$$- \ 12.70$$

9.
$$15.08$$
$$46.09$$
$$+ \ 145.73$$

10.
$$35.33$$
$$19.38$$
$$+ \ 10.94$$

11.
$$19.44$$
$$- \ 11.79$$

12.
$$99.421$$
$$- \ 77.025$$

An indirect object precedes the direct object in a sentence and tells *to whom* or *for whom* the action of the verb is done. Underline the verb in each sentence. Circle each indirect object.

13. José gave his puppy a bath.

14. Peter wished his grandmother a happy birthday.

15. Walter sold Yow the tire swing.

16. The waiter handed Kent his dinner plate.

17. Quinn offered Tommy her pencil.

18. Aunt May knitted June a yellow scarf.

19. Mr. Slider gave the chair a coat of varnish.

20. The students wrote their state representative a letter.

21. Our new neighbor brought our family some fresh vegetables.

DAY 6

Use the clue to unscramble each idiom. Write the idiom on the line.

22.   There can be many ways of doing something.

   lead roads Rome all to

   _____

23.   forced to decide between unpleasant choices

   and between hard rock a place a

   _____

24.   unable to think of a word that you know

   of the tongue on tip your

   _____

25.   to hear something and then immediately forget it

   the in out ear one other and

   _____

26.   to accept more responsibility than you can handle

   chew more bite than can you off

   _____

Pick one character in any book that you have read or movie that you have seen. Explain why you would want to be friends with this character. Use another sheet of paper if you need more space.

_____

_____

_____

_____

_____

_____

FACTOID: A lion's age can be estimated by the color of its nose.

Place the decimal point in each answer.

1.	2.	3.	4.	5.
21.7	63.1	36.6	3.41	7.67
× 4.2	× 2.2	× 4.7	× 6.2	× 1.3
9 1 1 4	1 3 8 8 2	1 7 2 0 2	2 1 1 4 2	9 9 7 1

6.	7.	8.	9.	10.
21.43	18.72	24.062	62.003	18.417
× 3.04	× 2.17	× 1.3	× 1.4	× 0.2
6 5 1 4 7 2	4 0 6 2 2 4	3 1 2 8 0 6	8 6 8 0 4 2	3 6 8 3 4

An adjective describes a noun. An adjective formed from a proper noun is called a proper adjective. Circle the common and proper adjectives. Draw an arrow from each adjective to the noun it describes.

11. A wood-handled shovel leaned against the red wheelbarrow.

12. The filthy refrigerator needed to be scoured.

13. The luxury sheets were made of Egyptian cotton.

14. I have mint gum in my top drawer.

15. Ben ordered New England clam chowder at his favorite restaurant.

16. William Shakespeare is a famous English playwright.

17. The purple pen is leaking ink.

18. Zoë wore her Japanese kimono for the festival.

19. Did you see the Chinese dragon on the menu cover?

20. Five birds swooped through the warm air.

DAY 7

Personification is a literary device in which an author gives human characteristics or emotions, such as love, to something that is not human, such as the moon. Read each sentence and explain what is being personified.

21. Fortune smiled on us that bright summer morning. _____

_____

22. The clock in the tower sang the time to the townspeople. _____

_____

23. The wind whistled cheerfully through the iron gates. _____

_____

24. The daisies beside the road waved happily as I walked past them. _____

_____

25. The Marino family will go to the zoo if the weather permits. _____

_____

Match each definition with the correct human body system.

A. muscular
B. excretory
C. immune
D. skeletal
E. nervous
F. digestive
G. respiratory
H. circulatory

26. _____ allows the body to move

27. _____ breaks down food and absorbs nutrients

28. _____ protects against disease and infection

29. _____ controls bodily functions

30. _____ takes in oxygen and releases carbon dioxide

31. _____ supports the body

32. _____ uses blood to deliver nutrients and oxygen

33. _____ removes waste

FITNESS FLASH: Do 10 sit-ups.

* See page ii.

Solve each problem.

1. 2.8
× 34

2. 6.2
× 13

3. 3.7
× 65

4. 0.17
× 14

5. 0.52
× 26

6. 0.208
× 21

7. 302.6
× 83

8. 3.208
× 91

9. 0.43
× 18

10. 0.618
× 36

11. 214.4
× 17

12. 4.197
× 43

Adjectives that compare two nouns are called comparative adjectives. Adjectives that compare more than two nouns are called superlative adjectives. Write the comparative and superlative forms of each adjective.

		Comparative	Superlative
13.	happy		
14.	wise		
15.	fast		
16.	great		
17.	delicious		
18.	interesting		
19.	majestic		
20.	friendly		
21.	energetic		
22.	smart		
23.	tall		

Read the passage. Then, answer the questions.

First, the Lightning

Lightning is a powerful force of nature. A single bolt of lightning is hotter than the surface of the sun. Although its formation is similar to a spark of static electricity, a lightning strike releases a tremendous amount of energy.

During a storm, small particles in clouds collect either positive or negative charges of energy. The lighter, positively charged particles rise to the top of the clouds. The heavier, negatively charged particles fall to the bottom of the clouds. This separation creates a path through the air for the flow of electricity. Once the attraction between the two groups becomes too strong, the particles release their stored energy. This electrical discharge is lightning.

The thunder that follows lightning is the sound made by the air as the lightning heats it. Lightning can instantly heat air molecules to more than 50,000°F (27,760°C). These heated molecules then expand and collide. This explosion of air is the source of the sound waves that we call thunder.

Although it seems like lightning and thunder occur at different times, this is only a trick of the senses. Light travels much faster than sound. This difference in speed explains why lightning and thunder reach us at different times. The sound of thunder takes more time than the light from a lightning strike to travel the same distance.

24. What is the sound of thunder? _____

_____

25. Why do we see lightning first and hear thunder later? _____

_____

26. Which of these statements is true?
    A. A lightning strike can be as hot as 1,000,000°F (555,538°C).
    B. Light travels at one-fifth the speed of sound.
    C. Negatively charged particles rise to the top of a cloud.
    D. A single bolt of lightning is hotter than the surface of the sun.

27. What is the main difference between a lightning strike and static electricity?

_____

FACTOID: More than 30 million people live in and around Tokyo, Japan.

Solve each problem.

1. A covered wagon on the Oregon Trail could travel about 2.5 miles per hour on flat terrain. About how many miles could it travel in 9 hours?

2. In 1860, gingham cloth sold for $0.25 per yard. Mrs. Olsen bought 16.4 yards to make clothes for her family. How much did she spend on cloth?

3. In 1863 in Fort Laramie, Wyoming, travelers could buy beef jerky at the trading post for $0.35 per pound. How much would a 16-pound box of beef jerky cost?

4. Each wagon in the Parley Company of Travelers wagon train was about 3.65 meters long. If 12 wagons traveled end to end, how long would the wagon train be?

A demonstrative adjective tells which item is being described. Circle the demonstrative adjective in each sentence and draw an arrow to the noun it describes.

5. Those scented candles produce very hot wax.

6. That four-year-old child chatters constantly.

7. This fuzzy peach has a bruised spot.

8. Those majestic glaciers tower above the cruise ship.

9. That dirty blue sock has a small hole in the toe.

10. This yellow pencil has a broken point.

11. My little sister is in that class.

12. Barney wants that chocolate cupcake with white frosting.

13. Vera drew this sketch of the storm clouds.

14. These tiny seeds can grow into delicious radishes.

DAY 9

Write each literary term from the word bank on the line next to its definition.

allusion	conflict	dialogue
foreshadowing	hyperbole	imagery
irony	point of view	setting

15. _____ the struggle within the story

16. _____ a reference to a real or fictitious person, place, or event

17. _____ spoken conversation between two characters

18. _____ exaggeration for effect

19. _____ using hints or clues to suggest what might happen later in a story

20. _____ the perspective from which a story is told

21. _____ the time and place in which a story occurs

22. _____ the use of words that mean the opposite of what one intends

23. _____ the use of descriptive language to help readers form vivid mental pictures

Integrity means having sound moral principles and being honest. Read the situation. On a separate sheet of paper, write a possible consequence of not demonstrating integrity. Then, write a benefit received for showing integrity.

You are the catcher on a softball team that is in a big game. If you win, your team will be in first place. A player from the other team is sprinting toward home plate. The ball is thrown to you. You catch the ball but just miss tagging the player sliding into home. The umpire has a blocked view and hesitates for a moment before calling the other team's player out.

FITNESS FLASH: Do 10 squats.

* See page ii.

Solve each problem.

1. $2\overline{)45.4}$ 2. $2\overline{)4.5}$ 3. $7\overline{)34.37}$ 4. $5\overline{)0.105}$

5. $6\overline{)120.6}$ 6. $6\overline{)12.06}$ 7. $4\overline{)2.44}$ 8. $6\overline{)2.76}$

The adjectives *a*, *an*, and *the* are called articles. Write *a* or *an* in front of each singular noun. Write *the* in front of each plural noun.

9. _____ employee   10. _____ architect

11. _____ doctor   12. _____ rangers

13. _____ professional 14. _____ students

15. _____ actress   16. _____ musicians

17. _____ monarchs   18. _____ forester

19. _____ candidates   20. _____ operator

21. _____ designer   22. _____ gymnast

23. _____ official   24. _____ instructors

DAY 10

Read the descriptions of waking up at Frog Pond. Then, answer the questions.

Camper One
We woke this morning to waves lapping the shore, a breeze rustling the leaves, and frogs croaking. They woke the geese and ducks, who sang good morning to the animals around the pond. Soon, all of the insects, birds, and animals were calling good morning to one another. How could I stay in bed? I needed to greet the morning too.

Camper Two
We woke this morning to the incessant croaking of frogs. This triggered off-key honking and quacking from around the pond. Waves slapped the shore, and the wind roared through the trees. Soon, the insects, birds, and animals were loudly protesting the hour. With all of this noise, it was hardly worth trying to go back to sleep.

25. How does Camper One feel about waking up at Frog Pond? _____

_____

26. How does Camper Two feel about waking up at Frog Pond? _____

_____

27. Write two facts from what happened at Frog Pond that morning. _____

_____

_____

Anagrams are formed by rearranging the letters in a word to create a new word. Find an anagram for each word. Some words may have more than one anagram.

28. felt _____   29. snap _____

30. atom _____   31. hose _____

32. crate _____   33. wasp _____

34. emit _____   35. pier _____

36. prod _____   37. grin _____

38. life _____   39. asleep _____

CHARACTER CHECK: Write five things that you are grateful for. Share your list with an adult.

Solve each problem.

1. $0.6\overline{)5.4}$ 2. $0.9\overline{)0.18}$ 3. $1.4\overline{)13.86}$ 4. $0.86\overline{)0.688}$

5. $1.7\overline{)10.54}$ 6. $2.4\overline{)16.8}$ 7. $0.07\overline{)0.035}$ 8. $0.92\overline{)0.736}$

Circle each adverb. Draw an arrow to the word it modifies. Then, write *how*, *where*, or *when* to indicate how the adverb modifies the word.

9. _____ Grace always finishes her papers.

10. _____ Addie often reminds us to buckle our seat belts.

11. _____ The exhausted children went inside.

12. _____ Lane frequently drinks milk with his meals.

13. _____ Clare and Mallory read outside in the summer.

14. _____ Juan played the music quietly.

15. _____ Winnie will work on her painting tonight.

16. _____ She quickly made a fruit salad.

17. _____ The storm wildly pounded the windows.

DAY 11

Read the passage. Then, answer the questions.

Regions of North America

North America has several geographic regions. In the far north of Canada is the tundra, characterized by frozen land and very cold temperatures. Canada also has areas of plains, forests, and mountains. Each region has particular animals that live there. While the plains are inhabited by animals such as geese and caribou, the forests include animals like the lynx, which likes to remain hidden.

Regions of the United States range from desert to grassland to forest. The western and southwestern states of Nevada, California, New Mexico, and Arizona have deserts that are home to rattlesnakes and roadrunners. The Great Plains covers the central United States and extends to Canada. A forested region extends from the Great Lakes to the Gulf of Mexico and is home to animals such as the black bear. Mexico has areas of deserts, tropical forests, and mountains. North America is a great place to see the diversity of nature.

18. What is the main idea of this passage?
    A. North America has many geographic regions.
    B. The lynx likes to remain hidden.
    C. The Southwestern United States has many deserts.

19. What is the tundra region like? _____

    _____

20. Where are deserts found in the United States? _____

    _____

21. What area does the Great Plains cover? _____

    _____

22. Which geographic regions exist in Mexico?

    _____

> **FACTOID:** When Orville Wright made the first successful airplane flight, he stayed in the air for approximately 12 seconds.

Write each fraction as a decimal.

1. $\frac{4}{5} =$

2. $\frac{3}{8} =$

3. $\frac{3}{5} =$

4. $\frac{9}{15} =$

5. $\frac{19}{25} =$

6. $\frac{17}{20} =$

7. $\frac{1}{25} =$

8. $\frac{9}{40} =$

9. $\frac{18}{25} =$

10. $\frac{3}{16} =$

Draw a line through each incorrect adverb. Write the correct adverb above each incorrect word.

Motion on the Moon

On August 2, 1971, Commander David R. Scott stood proud on the surface of the moon. As the cameras rolled, the astronaut dramatic dropped a feather and a hammer. On Earth, the hammer would fall much fast. Amazing, the two objects landed on the moon's surface at the same time. Unbelievable, Galileo Galilei had accurate predicted the results of this experiment near 400 years earlier. A legend claims that Galileo bold dropped a cannonball and a musket ball from the Leaning Tower of Pisa in Pisa, Italy, to test his theory, but few modern historians actual believe the tale.

DAY 12

Identify the setting in each situation. Write the place and circle the time.

11. Heath studies the *Tyrannosaurus rex* display at The Field Museum in Chicago, Illinois, and writes several answers on his field trip questionnaire.

Where? _____

When?   in the past   in the present   in the future

12. Jill was exhausted. She woke at sunup to cook breakfast over the campfire and load the wagon. Then, she got in line with the other wagons. Eight hours later, she was still sitting on the buckboard, trying to guide the oxen. She hoped that the place called California was worth the three-month trip.

Where? _____

When?   in the past   in the present   in the future

13. Luis sat at his desk. He was bored. He had heard the history lesson about the wars of the 1900s many times. After all, they happened more than 600 years ago.

Where? _____

When?   in the past   in the present   in the future

What is one talent or skill that you possess? How can you develop it into a career? Use another sheet of paper if you need more space.

_____

_____

_____

_____

_____

_____

 FITNESS FLASH: Do five push-ups.

* See page ii.

Write each decimal as a fraction or a mixed number. Simplify if possible.

1. 0.1 =

2. 2.6 =

3. 0.4 =

4. 6.5 =

5. 0.20 =

6. 0.25 =

7. 0.55 =

8. 6.34 =

9. 8.08 =

10. 0.04 =

11. 0.01 =

12. 4.06 =

13. 2.500 =

14. 0.505 =

15. 3.404 =

16. 0.532 =

Combine each pair of sentences using a coordinating conjunction from the word bank.

and	but	for	or	so	yet

17. Devin went swimming in the pool. He did not go swimming in the lake.

_____

_____

18. She enjoys making art. She chooses to spend more time playing sports.

_____

_____

19. Josie picked up her backpack. She got on the bus.

_____

_____

20. We can watch the movie. We can meet Joe at the park.

_____

_____

DAY 13

You can help preserve the environment around you. In the *cause* column of the chart, read how people have helped plants and animals. In the *effect* column, write how each cause helped the local environment.

Cause	Effect
Milkweed grows in a field but will be destroyed this winter when houses are built. Monarch butterflies lay their eggs on milkweed plants, and monarch caterpillars eat the plants. In the fall, Judy gathered some milkweed seeds. She got her parents' permission to plant the seeds in their backyard.	
David and his dad were canoeing in the creek. David saw a bird caught in a net on the shore. He and his dad rescued the bird and took it to a veterinarian. The veterinarian removed the bird from the net and threw the net in the trash.	

"Step-Up" to Fitness

A "step-up" is a strength exercise that uses the weight of your body to strengthen the hamstrings and quadriceps, two large muscle groups in your legs. For this exercise, you will need a sturdy, low footstool and a few minutes three or four days a week.

Stand in front of your footstool. Place your right foot firmly on the footstool. Push through your right foot to lift your body onto the footstool. Stand with both feet on the footstool. Then, leading with your right foot, carefully step down to the starting position. Keep your back straight and your abdominal muscles tight. Switch feet and repeat the exercise. Do two sets of 8–10 repetitions for each leg.

> **FACTOID:** An adult human's intestines are about 20 feet (6.1 m) long.

* See page ii.

Write each fraction as a percentage. Write each percentage as a fraction in lowest terms.

1. $\dfrac{3}{5} =$

2. $\dfrac{9}{10} =$

3. $\dfrac{13}{100} =$

4. $\dfrac{89}{100} =$

5. $4\% =$

6. $16\% =$

7. $25\% =$

8. $34\% =$

Correlative conjunctions join similar words, phrases, or clauses. Circle the correlative conjunctions in each sentence.

9. Last night, both Dion and Noreen won awards.

10. Just as cars follow street signs, so must bikes.

11. Neither the map nor the itinerary fit in Ophelia's scrapbook.

12. We could use either molasses or sugar to sweeten the cookies.

13. Bea not only decorated the cupcakes but also made them from scratch.

14. Neither Carlos nor Mirabel is going to the meeting tonight.

15. Either a period or a semicolon can correct a run-on sentence.

16. Whether it rains or not, we will play soccer.

17. Both the paper and the project are due on Friday.

18. Mr. Oliver said that I can either bring my own pencil or borrow one.

DAY 14

Read the passage. Then, answer the questions.

The Klondike Gold Rush

The Klondike Gold Rush was named after a river where a large deposit of gold was found in 1896. The Klondike River is located near Dawson City in Canada's Yukon Territory. People who wanted to travel from Alaska to Canada in search of gold had to bring one year's worth of supplies with them because there were no places along the way to get more supplies. They often spent time in Edmonton, Canada, stocking up on food, tools, and clothing for the journey.

The gold rush helped develop new towns in western Canada and the Pacific Northwest of the United States. In addition to thousands of prospectors, or people who searched for gold, the gold rush drew many professionals, such as doctors and teachers, who were needed in the new settlements. Today, the Klondike Gold Rush International Historical Park, which includes sites in both Canada and the United States, helps people remember the dreams of the prospectors and the difficulties they faced.

19. What is the main idea of this passage?
    A. Only a few people became rich during the gold rush.
    B. The Klondike Gold Rush brought many new people to Canada.
    C. Dawson City is located in the Yukon Territory.

20. What was the Klondike Gold Rush named after? _____

_____

21. What did people need to bring with them when traveling from Alaska

to Canada? _____

_____

22. What did people often do in Edmonton? _____

_____

23. Where did new towns develop during the gold rush? _____

_____

FITNESS FLASH: Do 10 lunges.

* See page ii.

Write each decimal as a percentage.

1. 0.37 =   2. 0.69 =   3. 0.40 =   4. 0.21 =

5. 0.999 =   6. 0.499 =   7. 1.75 =   8. 2.25 =

Write each percentage as a decimal.

9. 24% =   10. 65% =   11. 88% =   12. 3% =

13. 17% =   14. 9% =   15. 10% =   16. 86% =

An interjection is a word or phrase that shows surprise or another emotion. Underline each interjection and the punctuation following it.

17. OK, I understand this now.

18. Shh! We're trying to get our work done.

19. Ouch, get off my foot!

20. Wow! I passed!

21. Mmmm, something smells delicious!

22. Really, would you do that for me?

23. Stop! That isn't very nice.

24. Hold on, I'm almost finished.

25. Oops! I broke the lead on another pencil.

26. Hey, give that back!

DAY 15

Read the paragraph. Then, answer the questions.

Stars and Planets

Stars and planets are types of objects in outer space. They are far from Earth and look like bright specks in the night sky. A planet is solid, but a star is a ball of hot gases. Planets absorb light from the sun, while stars produce their own light. Stars are extremely hot, but planets can be any temperature.

27. What two things does this paragraph compare? _____

28. How are the two things similar? How are they different? _____

_____

_____

Write the letter of each biome from the word bank next to its description. You will use some biomes more than once.

A.	deciduous forest	B.	desert	C.	grassland
D.	taiga	E.	tropical rain forest	F.	tundra

29. _____ has the largest diversity of animal and plant life

30. _____ has evergreen trees that can stand cold temperatures

31. _____ has a canopy of trees that lets little light reach the understory

32. _____ has many types of deciduous trees

33. _____ has animals, such as hawks, deer, moose, and wolves

34. _____ has very little rainfall

35. _____ has animals, such as zebras, lions, rhinoceroses, and owls

36. _____ has animals, such as insects, spiders, reptiles, and birds

37. _____ has tall grasses that provide food and shelter for animals

38. _____ has animals, such as squirrels, rabbits, wolves, and bears

39. _____ has permafrost that is frozen year-round

CHARACTER CHECK: Look up the word *reliable* in a dictionary. How are you reliable?

Find the percentage of each number.

1. 3% of 10 =	2. 4% of 30 =	3. 16% of 80 =
4. 18% of 36 =	5. 6% of 80 =	6. 9% of 90 =
7. 8% of 68 =	8. 9% of 75 =	9. 62% of 62 =
10. 4% of 400 =	11. 3% of 200 =	12. 37% of 51 =

Circle the prepositions in each sentence.

13.   Gracie and Helen had not seen each other for 50 years.

14.   "Tell me about Grandpa," said Randy.

15.   They carried the water packs on their backs.

16.   I would go into the garden, but it is muddy.

17.   Tommy passed the peas to his mother.

18.   We should meet somewhere beyond the city limits.

19.   The lights activate automatically after sunset.

20.   Please put an umbrella in the trunk.

21.   Add pepper to the soup.

22.   Erika waded into the stream and looked at the minnows.

Read the paragraph. Then, answer the questions.

Biographies and Mysteries

Biographies and mysteries are both types of books. A biography contains facts about a person's life. It might be written by that person or by someone else. A mystery is usually fictional. It describes how a puzzle or problem is solved by a detective, a police officer, or another person.

23.   What two things does this paragraph compare? _____

24.   How are the two things similar? How are they different? _____

_____

Read the passage. Draw a line to match each of the statue's features with its meaning.

The Statue of Liberty

In 1884, France gave the United States a statue named *Liberty Enlightening the World*. The statue celebrated the spirit of liberty and the friendship between the two countries. It stands near the former immigration station at Ellis Island, where it greeted millions of immigrants who entered the United States. The statue became known as the Statue of Liberty, and it has come to represent freedom and opportunity.

The statue stands on Liberty Island in New York City, New York. It was originally designed to serve as a lighthouse. However, when the torch was lit, its light was too dim to see from far away. After a renovation in 1986, the torch was rebuilt and covered in gold leaf.

25.   broken chain at her feet   A.   the light of liberty

26.   crown with seven spikes   B.   seven seas and continents

27.   shining torch   C.   the Roman goddess of liberty

28.   flowing robe   D.   breaking free from tyranny

29.   July IV, MDCCLXXVI on the tablet   E.   book of law that holds everything together

30.   tablet in the shape of a keystone   F.   date the Declaration of Independence was signed

FACTOID: Most of Indonesia's approximately 13,000 islands are uninhabited by people.

Complete the table.

	Regular Price	Discount Rate	Discount	Sale Price
1.	$24	40%		
2.	$25	30%		
3.	$80	15%		
4.	$220	60%		
5.	$90	55%		
6.	$120	45%		
7.	$1,250	25%		

Underline each prepositional phrase. Circle the object of each preposition. There may be more than one prepositional phrase in each sentence.

8.   We finally found shelter from the weather.

9.   In the afternoon, we drove toward Memphis, Tennessee.

10.   Until that point, everything had gone well.

11.   Cody used the key to his parents' house that was hidden under the birdbath.

12.   The new dog in our neighborhood has tags on its collar.

13.   My desk is covered with junk mail.

14.   Dad slept through the show.

15.   In place of nails, I used screws.

16.   There were boulders and rocks beside the bridge.

DAY 17

Read the passage. Then, answer the questions.

The Rosetta Stone

The Rosetta Stone was found among ruins in Egypt more than 200 years ago. It unlocked the mystery of the symbols that cover the temples and tombs of Ancient Egypt. The Rosetta Stone was carved and displayed for people to read in approximately 196 BC. It was named after the place where it was found, a town called Rosetta in what is today the country of Egypt.

There are three different kinds of writing on the stone. The writing on the top part of the stone consists of rows of small pictures, called hieroglyphics. Hieroglyphics were often carved on walls or on slabs of stone. The Egyptian priests used hieroglyphics. The second kind of writing on the stone is now known as **demotic**, or popular, script. It was used by the Greeks in their everyday writing—for example, to send messages. The third section, located at the bottom of the stone, is written in Greek. By 196 BC, a Greek family named the Ptolemys had been ruling Egypt for over 100 years. Because of this, the Greek alphabet and language were being used in Egypt along with Egyptian writing.

17.   What is the main idea of the first paragraph? _____

   _____

   _____

18.   What is the main idea of the second paragraph? _____

   _____

   _____

19.   What is the main idea of the entire passage? _____

   _____

   _____

20.   Which of the following best defines the word *demotic*?
   A.   angry   B.   popular
   C.   written in stone   D.   language

FITNESS FLASH: Do 10 squats.

Continue each number pattern.

1. 5, 8, 11, 14, 17, ____ , ____ , ____

2. 91, 86, 81, 76, 71, ____ , ____ , ____

3. 100, 92, 84, 76, 68, ____ , ____ , ____

4. 10, 20, 25, 35, 40, ____ , ____ , ____

5. 72, 69, 66, 63, 60, ____ , ____ , ____

6. 317, 402, 487, 572, ____ , ____ , ____

7. 5, 11, 23, 41, 65, ____ , ____ , ____

8. 244, 226, 208, 190, ____ , ____ , ____

9. 1, 4, 9, 16, 25, ____ , ____ , ____

10. 1, 2, 4, 8, 16, ____ , ____ , ____

Write the part of speech of each boldfaced word.

11. The roof **on** the old barn is peeling. _____

12. A row of ants **marched** across the picnic blanket. _____

13. My **mom** loves to visit Montreal, Quebec. _____

14. Walter put on his boots before going **outside**. _____

15. Taylor and her parents are driving to **Oregon**. _____

16. Evan wants to visit France, **and** Brianna wants to visit Italy. _____

17. Samantha bought **three** peaches at the store. _____

18. Kobe often **eats** lunch with his friend Victoria. _____

19. Is **he** going to the store with Jamil? _____

20. **The** dance will take place in the school gym. _____

Read each sentence. If the sentence contains faulty reasoning, explain why the reasoning is illogical. If it does not contain faulty reasoning, write *logical*.

21. Children over the age of 12 were admitted, so Ashley, age 13, and Bryan, age 14, were allowed in, while Fern, age 6, would have to wait. _____

_____

22. Every time I carry a green and purple umbrella, it rains. Therefore, if I carry a green and purple umbrella tomorrow, it will rain. _____

_____

23. Lamar waters his lawn on even-numbered days. So, on odd-numbered days, he keeps his sprinklers off. _____

_____

Write the letter of each type of renewable energy next to its description.

| A. biomass | B. geothermal | C. hydroelectric |
| D. solar | E. tidal | F. wind |

24. _____ uses the steam and hot water produced by energy within Earth to operate power plants and heat homes

25. _____ burns organic material from plants to produce steam for making electricity or heating homes; can also be made into automobile fuel

26. _____ uses the daily rising and falling of ocean levels to power turbines that spin a generator to create electricity

27. _____ directs flowing water through a turbine that spins a generator to create electricity

28. _____ photovoltaic cells convert the sun's radiation into usable electricity

29. _____ fast-moving air turns turbines that spin a generator to create electricity

FACTOID: There are more than 900 species of bats in the world.

Solve each equation.

1. $y + 8 = 11$ 2. $x + 8 = 24$ 3. $v + 3 = 13$ 4. $m + 12 = 18$

5. $q - 15 = 100$ 6. $r - 19 = 37$ 7. $w - 32 = 32$ 8. $z - 12 = 29$

9. $a + 7 = 20$ 10. $y - 22 = 45$ 11. $g + 15 = 31$ 12. $c - 83 = 24$

Read each sentence. Draw a line through each modifier that needs to be removed. If a new modifier is needed, write it on the line.

13. We don't hardly have time to watch television. _____

14. Your answer doesn't make no difference to her. _____

15. My sisters work even more harder than I do. _____

16. Kobe does good in all of his subjects at school. _____

17. Benny is tallest than me. _____

18. There are so many choices that I don't know which one I like more. _____

19. I couldn't hardly believe that my parents let me get a dog. _____

20. This cake is gooder than the pie that you bought. _____

21. He is one of the most funniest people I know. _____

22. This painting is more prettier than that one. _____

DAY 19

Read each question and evaluate how you would answer it. Use the key to write the level of your answer on the line.

Level 1 = yes or no response	Level 2 = one-word or short answer	Level 3 = extended answer

23. _____ Where is the Grand Canyon?

24. _____ How does a virus invade the body?

25. _____ How do you make chocolate chip cookies?

26. _____ Where do anemones live?

27. _____ Do people float in space?

28. _____ How is energy delivered from the dam to houses?

29. _____ What is the name of the winning football team?

30. _____ How does a spider make a web?

31. _____ When do monarch butterflies migrate?

32. _____ Do cheetahs run faster than gazelles?

33. _____ When is soccer season?

34. _____ Will you study for the test with me?

You have been offered a round-trip ride in a time machine and can travel any distance into the past. What time period would you want to travel to? Why? Use another sheet of paper if you need more space.

_____

_____

_____

_____

_____

FITNESS FLASH: Do 10 sit-ups.

* See page ii.

In descending order, list the four rules that apply to the order of operations.

_____

_____

_____

_____

Use the order of operations to simplify each math expression. Write a number expression for each phrase below. Then, solve each equation.

1. $28 \div 7 + 10 =$ _____

2. $6 \times 2 + 6 \times 3 =$ _____

3. $40 - 3 \times 4 + 5 =$ _____

4. $(10 - 4) \times 3 - 10 =$ _____

5. $9 + 6 - 12 + 8 =$ _____

6. $(7 + 2) \div (7 - 4) =$ _____

Write _I_ if the group of words is an independent clause. Write _D_ if the group of words is a dependent clause.

7. _____ whenever Dillon receives a letter

8. _____ everyone encourages him

9. _____ Jasmine rides her horse, Tally

10. _____ so Chad bought a new hat

11. _____ those flowers are blooming early

12. _____ until Lila finishes her homework

13. _____ I walked one mile before school

14. _____ since it was lightning and thundering

DAY 20

Read the passage. Then, answer the questions.

Constellations

Constellations are patterns of stars that are visible in the night sky. Some constellations are named after animals, and others are named after mythical characters. Although stars in a constellation may look close together, they are actually very far apart. Brighter stars are closer to Earth, and dimmer stars are farther away.

The International Astronomical Union (IAU) recognizes 88 official constellations. One of the best-known constellations is the Big Dipper. The stars appear to form the handle and bowl of a water dipper. The Big Dipper is part of a larger constellation known as Ursa Major, or the Great Bear.

People in different parts of the world see different parts of the night sky. Different constellations are also visible at different times of the year. However, some constellations can be seen by people in both hemispheres. The constellation of Orion, the Hunter, is visible in both the Northern and Southern Hemispheres, but in the Southern Hemisphere, it appears upside down!

15. What is the main idea of this passage?
    A. Constellations are patterns of stars that are present in the night sky.
    B. Some stars are very far from Earth.
    C. Australia is located in the Southern Hemisphere.

16. What are constellations named for? _____

_____

17. Why do some stars appear brighter than others?

_____

_____

18. What is the IAU? _____

19. What do the stars of the Big Dipper appear to form?

_____

_____

CHARACTER CHECK: Keep a tally through the day of the number of times you show consideration. Share the results with a family member.

Bending Light

How is light refracted, or bent, as it passes through transparent objects, such as glass and water?

Materials:
- coins, pebbles, and similar small objects that sink
- clear drinking glass filled with water
- flashlight
- masking tape
- pencil
- sharpened pencil
- small aquarium or clear rectangular container

Procedure:
Place the pencil in the glass of water and observe it from different angles. Then, fill the aquarium or clear rectangular container with water. Place various objects that sink, such as coins or pebbles, in the water. Look at these objects from the side, from above, and at an angle. Cover the front of the flashlight with several layers of masking tape. Poke a hole near the center of the tape with the sharpened pencil. When you turn on the flashlight, a thin beam of light should shine through the hole. Turn off the lights in the room. Focus the light into the aquarium from the side, from above, and at different angles.

1. Describe what you saw when you observed the pencil in the glass of water.

   _____

   _____

   _____

2. Describe what you saw when you looked at the coins, pebbles, or other objects in the aquarium from the side, from above, and at different angles. _____

   _____

   _____

3. Describe what you saw when you shone the light into the aquarium from the side, from above, and at different angles. _____

   _____

   _____

BONUS

Lifting with Air!

Is air pressure strong enough to lift heavy objects?

Even though gases like oxygen and carbon dioxide are invisible, they still exert pressure on objects around them. In this activity, you will test the strength of air pressure.

Materials:
- 1-gallon resealable plastic bag
- 3–4 books
- duct or packaging tape
- plastic drinking straw
- sharpened pencil

Procedure:
Seal the plastic bag. Place one book on top of the bag and leave about 2" (5 cm) of the bottom of the bag showing beneath the book. Use the sharpened pencil to poke a hole in the bag. Place the drinking straw in the hole. Use the tape to seal the space around the straw so that no air can escape. Blow into the straw. When you need to take a breath, place your finger over the end of the straw to keep air from leaking out. Blow into the bag until it is partially inflated. Observe what happens to the book when you blow into the bag. Then, place two or three books on top of the first book and continue to blow into the straw.

1. What happened to the book when you blew into the bag? _____

_____

_____

2. Was the air pressure strong enough to lift several books? _____

_____

3. Write one property of air that allows it to lift objects. _____

_____

4. Can you think of another situation in which air pressure is strong enough to lift a

heavy object? _____

_____

_____

_____

Country, Region, or City?

Identify each place as a country, a region, or a city. Then, choose one place to research. Write three facts about the place you chose. Use reference resources if you need help.

1. Egypt _____

2. Dublin _____

3. Costa Rica _____

4. South Pacific _____

5. Oslo _____

6. Canberra _____

7. Belize _____

8. Panama _____

9. Middle East _____

10. Argentina _____

11. Japan _____

12. Great Plains _____

13. Florence _____

14. Pacific Northwest _____

15. Saudi Arabia _____

16. Montreal _____

17. Kenya _____

18. Austria _____

19. Kathmandu _____

20. Arctic Circle _____

_____

_____

_____

BONUS

Geography Terms

Use the geography terms from the word bank to solve the crossword puzzle.

canyon
cape
delta
dune
glacier
isthmus
lagoon
mesa
oasis
pampas
plateau
reservoir
savanna
steppes
strait
tributary

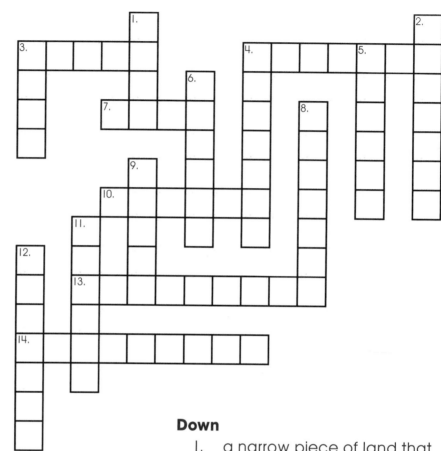

Across

3. roughly triangular land at the mouth of a river formed from deposits of silt
4. semi-dry plains with sparse vegetation
7. Spanish for *table*; steep-sided, flat-topped land
10. water partially or completely enclosed within an atoll
13. water-holding site
14. smaller river or stream that flows into a larger one

Down

1. a narrow piece of land that projects into a body of water
2. narrow strip of land connecting two larger land masses
3. a sandy hill formed by the wind
4. flat, open grassland with scattered trees and shrubs
5. Argentina's flat, grassy plains
6. steep-sided, narrow, deep valley
8. large, slow-moving sheet of ice
9. in a desert, a fertile area with a steady water supply
11. narrow body of water connecting two larger bodies of water
12. large, high, flat area that rises above the surrounding land

North and Central America

Use the letters from the map to identify the following North and Central American countries. Then, choose a country and use reference resources to answer the questions.

1. _____ El Salvador

2. _____ Greenland

3. _____ Belize

4. _____ United States

5. _____ Nicaragua

6. _____ Canada

7. _____ Mexico

8. _____ Guatemala

9. _____ Honduras

10. _____ Panama

11. _____ Costa Rica

12. _____ Cuba

13. _____ Jamaica

14. _____ Haiti

15. _____ Dominican Republic

16. _____ Bahamas

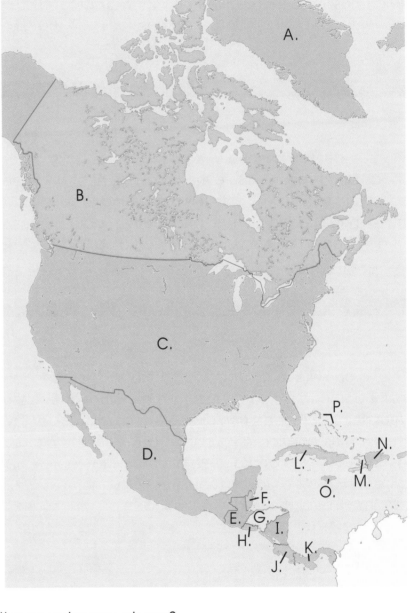

17. What is the population of the country you chose? _____

18. What form of government does this country have? _____

19. What is the country's capital? _____

BONUS

Take It Outside!

Have a family member join you on a walk around a community park. Bring a pen and a notebook. Record the geographical features you observe in the park, such as streams, rivers, boulders, and hills. Once you return home, make a list of at least 10 prepositions. Then, reflect on your walk around the park. Write a short story or poem about the walk. Incorporate prepositions with the geographical features that you saw.

Go outside with a friend or family member. Take a pencil, a notebook, and a measuring tape. Measure the area in front of and behind where you live. Having someone to help you with the measuring tape will make the task easier. After you have measured the length and width of both places, determine the total area in front of and behind where you live. Which area is larger? How much larger is it?

Take a camera, a notebook, and a pen and go for a walk around your neighborhood with an adult. Take a picture of each landmark or notable place in your neighborhood, such as your home, school, or favorite restaurant. Record each landmark's location in your notebook. Print the pictures when you return home. On a piece of posterboard, create a map that represents your neighborhood. Tape or glue your pictures to the map. Beneath each picture, write a brief description of each landmark or place and why it is shown on your map.

Monthly Goals

Think of three goals to set for yourself this month. For example, you may want to learn five new vocabulary words each week. Write your goals on the lines. Post them someplace visible, where you will see them every day.

Place a check mark next to each goal that you complete. Feel proud that you have met your goals and set new ones to continue to challenge yourself.

1. _____
2. _____
3. _____

Word List

The following words are used in this section. Use a dictionary to look up each word that you do not know. Then, write three sentences. Use at least one word from the word list in each sentence.

abash	occupations
census	pharaohs
demographic	precise
habitat	province
inhabitants	scholars

1. _____

   _____

2. _____

   _____

3. _____

   _____

Introduction to Endurance

This section includes fitness and character development activities that focus on endurance. These activities are designed to get you moving and thinking about developing your physical and mental stamina.

Physical Endurance

What do climbing stairs, jogging, and riding your bike have in common? They are all great ways to build endurance!

Having endurance means performing an activity for a period of time before your body becomes tired. Improving your endurance requires regular aerobic exercise, which causes your heart to beat faster. You also breathe harder. As a result of regular aerobic activity, your heart becomes stronger, and your blood cells deliver oxygen to your body more efficiently.

Summer provides numerous opportunities to improve your endurance. Although there are times when a relaxing activity is valuable, it is important to take advantage of the warm mornings and sunny days to go outside. Choose activities that you enjoy. Invite a family member on a walk or a bicycle ride. Play a game of basketball with friends. Leave the relaxing activities for when it is dark, too hot, or raining.

Set an endurance goal this summer. For example, you might jog every day until you can run one mile without stopping. Set new goals when you meet your old ones. Be proud of your endurance success!

Mental Endurance

Endurance applies to the mind as well as to the body. Showing mental endurance means sticking with something. You can show mental endurance every day. Staying with a task when you might want to quit and continuing until it is done are ways that you can show mental endurance.

Build your mental endurance this summer. Maybe you want to earn some extra money for a new bike by helping your neighbors with yard work. But, after one week of working in your neighbors' yards, you realize it is not as easy as you thought it would be. Think about some key points, such as how you have wanted that new bike for months. Be positive. Remind yourself that you have only been working for one week and that your neighbors are very appreciative of your work. Think of ways to make the yard work more enjoyable, such as starting earlier in the day or listening to music while you work. Quitting should be the last resort.

Build your mental endurance now. It will help prepare you for challenges you may face later.

Determine the probability that each event will happen. Simplify if possible.

A jar contains 18 marbles that are all the same size. It contains 7 purple marbles, 3 green marbles, and 8 orange marbles. Without looking, Travis chooses 1 marble. What is the probability of each of the following outcomes?

1. P(green) = _____   2. P(not green) = _____

3. P(purple) = _____   4. P(purple or green) = _____

5. P(orange) = _____   6. P(not orange) = _____

Draw a line from each dependent clause to the independent clause that completes the sentence.

dependent clause || **independent clause**

7. If you save your money,   A. Toto got a treat.

8. Because the leaves were changing colors   B. Jonah's stepfather took him to school.

9. When I see the street sign,   C. I know the movie is good.

10. From the large crowd of people,   D. we knew autumn was here.

11. Since his mother was sick,   E. you can buy a new video game.

12. Because he is a good dog,   F. I know to turn right.

13. but I had to leave early.   G. The game was exciting,

14. Write a dependent clause. _____

_____

15. Now, add an independent clause to the dependent clause to make a complete sentence. _____

_____

DAY 1

Write a definition for each word.

16. firm _____

17. coast _____

18. current _____

Write a definition for each boldfaced word as it is used in the sentence. Then, compare the definitions to your definitions above.

19. My brother works for a law **firm** in Chicago, Illinois. _____

_____

20. Hunter likes to **coast** down that large hill on his bike. _____

_____

21. Zaila let the **current** carry her kayak downstream. _____

_____

Historians study major events from the past, but they also study the lives of everyday people. To do this, historians study the objects and documents that people leave behind. Imagine that you are a historian from the future. What would you learn about 21st-century life from studying your home? Use another sheet of paper if you need more space.

_____

_____

_____

_____

_____

_____

_____

_____

FACTOID: Ninety percent of an iceberg lies beneath the surface of the water.

Determine the probability that each event will happen. Simplify if possible.

A die numbered 1 through 6 is rolled. Find the probability of each outcome.

1. P(5) = _____

2. P(1 or 2) = _____

3. P(odd number) = _____

4. P(not 6) = _____

5. P(even number) = _____

6. P(1, 2, 3, or 4) = _____

Each of the following sentences contains either a compound subject or a compound predicate. Circle the words that make up each compound subject. Underline the words that make each compound predicate.

7. Corn and green beans are my two favorite vegetables.

8. The game both entertained and excited the football fans.

9. Beth cooked her dinner and then ate it.

10. Diana and I cooked dinner for her parents.

11. Those attending the school picnic sipped lemonade and played games on the

    soccer field.

12. Vanilla and butter pecan are my two favorite flavors of ice cream.

13. Write a sentence about your family that has a compound subject.

    _____

    _____

    _____

14. Write a sentence about a close friend that has a compound predicate.

    _____

    _____

    _____

DAY 2

Write a definition for each word.

15. might _____

16. sling _____

17. hail _____

Write a definition for each boldfaced word as it is used in the sentence. Then, compare the definitions to your definitions above.

18. Leigh pushed against the bookcase with all of her **might**. _____

_____

19. The doctor put Terrance's sprained wrist in a **sling**. _____

_____

20. It is not always easy to **hail** a taxi in the city. _____

With which of your family members do you have the most in common? Describe the similarities between you and the person. What do you like to do together? Use another sheet of paper if you need more space.

_____

_____

_____

_____

_____

_____

_____

_____

 FITNESS FLASH: Jog in place for 30 seconds.

Solve the problem. Show your work in the space provided.

Mr. and Mrs. Jackson are having a family portrait taken with their son and daughter. The photographer wants to have two people sit in the front and two people stand in the back. The Jacksons have decided that they want to send a copy of their portrait to each of their relatives. However, they don't want any two portraits to be the same. Mr. Wilson has asked the photographer to place the family in as many different positions as possible.

1.   How many different portraits are possible? _____

Rewrite each sentence. Include apostrophes where they are needed.

2.   Phil isnt only a singer; hes also a drummer. _____

_____

_____

3.   Omars golf clubs didnt arrive, so he borrowed his friends set._____

_____

_____

4.   Jamies shoes were found in the gym, so shell need to pick them up from the

coachs office._____

_____

5.   If I study hard this semester, Im sure Ill get good grades. _____

_____

_____

6.   I thought that the kite was Noras, but she said that it was her sister-in-laws.

_____

_____

Read the passage. Then, answer the questions.

Demographics

Demographics are characteristics of human populations. The word *demographics* contains the word roots *demo*, meaning "people," and *graph*, meaning "to write." Demographic data includes people's ages, occupations, educational levels, and incomes. Government officials can use this information to determine the makeup of a city's or county's population and whether there is a need for different services. For example, if a city's officials learn that many families with young children are moving into the area, they may recommend building more schools.

One way that countries collect demographic data is by taking a national census. In the United States, an official census of the population is taken every 10 years. In Canada, a national census is taken every 5 years. Both countries use demographics to examine trends in their populations.

7. What is the main idea of this passage?
    A. Rural cities may have fewer residents than urban ones.
    B. Some cities have a large number of young people.
    C. Demographics include various information about people's lives.

8. What types of information might demographic data include? _____
    _____

9. How do government officials use demographic data? _____
    _____

10. How do countries collect demographic data?_____
    _____
    _____

11. How often are censuses taken in the United States and Canada?_____
    _____

FACTOID: President Lyndon B. Johnson was an elevator operator and a teacher before becoming president.

Find the mean, median, mode, and range of each set of data.

1. 34, 41, 33, 41, 31

    mean: _____   median: _____

    mode: _____   range: _____

2. 18, 10, 10, 8, 35, 10, 21

    mean: _____   median: _____

    mode: _____   range: _____

3. 7, 14, 10, 14, 29, 16, 15

    mean: _____   median: _____

    mode: _____   range: _____

4. 41, 18, 24, 41, 72, 82, 16

    mean: _____   median: _____

    mode: _____   range: _____

Add apostrophes where they are needed in the paragraph.

Family Friends

Camilles best friend is Marcella. Theyre in different classes this year, but theyve known each other since preschool. They havent spent more than a few days apart in their lives. Marcellas mom is Camilles fathers boss. Marcellas father is Camilles uncles business partner. The two families friendship has lasted more than 15 years. Marcella has two older brothers, and Camille has one. Theyre in high school now, but theyll be in college soon. The boys relationship is very close too. They dont hesitate to call one another for advice.

DAY 4

Read each sentence. Then, circle the letter next to the synonym for the boldfaced word. Use a dictionary if you need help.

5. The yearbook includes many **candid** shots of students.
   A. hidden
   B. athletic
   C. difficult
   D. unposed

6. The weather was **balmy** this morning, but it may rain this afternoon.
   A. mild
   B. windy
   C. chilly
   D. stormy

7. The tennis team was **exultant** after its win in the tournament.
   A. upset
   B. bored
   C. angry
   D. thrilled

8. Katie's new dog is **docile** and sweet.
   A. frightened
   B. nervous
   C. calm
   D. energetic

9. Louis's teacher said that Louis is responsible and **competent**.
   A. unhappy
   B. hungry
   C. mischievous
   D. capable

Sprint to Endurance

Interval training is one way to improve your endurance. With interval training, bursts of exercise are followed by short periods of recovery. For this exercise, you will need a pair of comfortable running shoes and a safe, flat place to run and walk.

To begin, jog for several minutes until your muscles are warm. Once you are ready, sprint for 10–15 seconds. Then, walk for 45–60 seconds. Alternate sprinting and walking until you have sprinted five times. Find landmarks, such as mailboxes and trees, to help you time your intervals. For example, you may want to sprint to a mailbox and then walk back, or sprint to a tree and then walk to the next tree before sprinting again.

FITNESS FLASH: Do 10 jumping jacks.

* See page ii.

Rather than interpreting data, create data to fit the conditions described in each situation. Show your work to prove that you have chosen valid data.

1. Create a set of data that contains 11 test scores and satisfies each condition below:

    Mean: 83

    Median: 81

    Mode: 80

    Range: 26

2. Create a set of data that shows temperature highs for 10 days and satisfies each condition below:

    Mean: 72°

    Median: 74°

    Mode: 68°

    Range: 21°

Write commas where they are needed in each sentence.

3. Gretchen can you give me a hand?

4. The mural was filled with splashes of blue green gold and red.

5. Mrs. Yim my fourth-grade teacher was always my favorite.

6. You can either come to my house or I will come to yours.

7. Carla donated food blankets and clothing.

8. "Please show me the way out of here" said Mia.

9. I want to leave but I am afraid that I will miss something.

10. On Saturday April 18 2009 I went swimming in Crystal Creek.

DAY 5

Read each summary. Underline the sentence that does not belong.

11. The topic of the article I read was rain forest plants. Animals like monkeys and sloths live in the rain forest. Numerous flowering plants and vines grow on the forest floor. Many of the trees grow to heights of city buildings. Bromeliads are plants that sometimes grow in the rain forest's canopy.

12. The article, "Today's Computers," describes the many uses of computers. They are used to access the Internet. Word processing programs are used for reports, letters, and schoolwork. They are also used for recreational and educational computer games. Some computers come in different colors.

Read each sentence. Write *M* if the situation describes mechanical weathering. Write *C* if the situation describes chemical weathering.

13. _____ Acid rain dissolves limestone.

14. _____ A large rock falls from a cliff and breaks.

15. _____ Water in the cracks of a rock freezes and breaks apart the rock.

16. _____ An old car sitting outside for several years forms rust on its underside.

17. _____ Tree roots crack the foundation of a house.

18. _____ Moss grows on the surface of a rock, producing pits.

19. _____ The edges of a rock become rounded over time as water carries it along the bottom of a stream.

20. _____ A marble gravestone in an area with high pollutants becomes difficult to read over time.

21. _____ Wind blows sand against a rock formation in the desert.

CHARACTER CHECK: Write a story about a character who demonstrates diligence.

Solve each problem.

1. In a sample, 11 out of 25 marbles are green. Predict approximately how many green marbles are in a box of 100 marbles.

2. In a sample, 54 out of 75 middle school students said that they are going to the school carnival. Based on this sample, approximately how many of the 750 middle school students are going to the carnival?

3. In a sample of 50 sixth-grade students, 32 students said that they are entering the school writing contest. Based on this sample, approximately how many of the school's 250 sixth graders will enter the writing contest?

4. In a sample, 25 sixth graders reported their T-shirt sizes. The results were: small–3, medium–9, and large–13. Approximately how many of each size should be ordered for 250 sixth graders?

Write commas where they are needed in the paragraph.

Jarvis and Rover

Jarvis is a kind helpful honest friend. He has short black hair and large brown friendly eyes. When I go to Jarvis's house, we play with his dog Rover. Rover is a gentle quiet dog. His tail is long thin and feathery. His ears are floppy soft and silky. They fly behind him when he runs. Rover is always ready to plant a big sloppy kiss on my cheek. Just like Jarvis Rover likes everybody and everybody likes him.

DAY 6

Read the passage. Then, answer the questions.

The Vikings in Canada

The Vikings were the first Europeans to cross the Atlantic Ocean and reach North America. Historians knew that the Vikings settled in Greenland and Iceland but were not sure how much time they spent in Canada. In 1960, a Viking settlement from around AD 1000 was found at L'Anse aux Meadows in what is now the Canadian province of Newfoundland and Labrador. Archaeologists uncovered the ruins of eight buildings that had sod walls and roofs over supporting frames. In the middle of each floor was a long, narrow fireplace used for heating and cooking. Archaeologists also found tools the Vikings had used. Because the design of the tools and the buildings was similar to those found in Viking settlements in Greenland and Iceland, it was clear that the Vikings settled in Canada as well. Today, L'Anse aux Meadows is a national historic site, and many people visit it each year.

5.   What is the main idea of this passage?
   A.   Archaeologists uncovered the ruins of eight buildings.
   B.   The first Europeans to reach North America were the Vikings.
   C.   Many people visit national historic sites each year.

6.   In which areas of North America did the Vikings settle?

   _____

7.   What was found in 1960 at L'Anse aux Meadows?

   _____

8.   What did the buildings at L'Anse aux Meadows look like?

   _____

   _____

9.   How did archaeologists know that it was a Viking settlement?

   _____

   _____

> **FACTOID:** Two stars that orbit each other are called *doubles* or *binary stars*. Half of the stars in the universe are doubles.

Write each ratio as a fraction.

1. 5 cheetahs to 7 tigers _____
2. 20 tulips to 13 roses _____
3. 12 trumpets to 5 violins _____
4. 4 taxis to 9 buses _____
5. Jill's 23¢ to Bob's 45¢ _____
6. 10 chairs to 3 tables _____
7. 1 meter to 4 meters _____
8. 3 minutes to 25 minutes _____

Use the information in the box to write each ratio as a fraction.

9. soccer balls to footballs _____
10. baseballs to soccer balls _____
11. footballs to baseballs _____
12. baseballs to all balls _____

Write quotation marks where they are needed in each sentence.

13. Morgan shouted, Hurray! We made it!
14. Have you been a part of a sports team at your school? asked Silvia.
15. After you take out the trash, said my dad, we can go see a movie.
16. Reid told Angie that Casey at the Bat was his favorite poem.
17. Look out for that bump in the road! shouted Dad.
18. Leave your binoculars at home, suggested Ms. Haynes. Your ears will be more helpful than your eyes on this field trip.
19. What is the quickest way to get to the park? asked Andre.
20. We are going to the movies this afternoon, said Deanna, and then we are going to get ice cream.
21. Be careful! shouted Mom.

DAY 7

Read the words in the word bank. Complete the outline by writing the subheadings and supporting details on the lines. Use each word or phrase once.

books	chairs	desks
furniture	library books	paper
pencils	pens	reference books
storage cabinets	supplies	textbooks

Classroom

A. _____

    1. _____

    2. _____

    3. _____

B. _____

    1. _____

    2. _____

    3. _____

C. _____

    1. _____

    2. _____

    3. _____

A primary source provides information about an event from someone who was present when the event occurred. A secondary source collects and interprets information from other sources after an event has happened. Read each description. Write *P* if the source is a primary source. Write *S* if the source is a secondary source.

22. _____ a diary

23. _____ an encyclopedia

24. _____ a textbook

25. _____ a photograph

26. _____ a biography

27. _____ a history book

28. _____ a letter

29. _____ a birth certificate

30. _____ an interview

31. _____ taped news footage

FITNESS FLASH: Hop on your left foot 10 times.

* See page ii.

Solve for each variable.

1. $\dfrac{5}{6} = \dfrac{n}{36}$

2. $\dfrac{3}{8} = \dfrac{x}{24}$

3. $\dfrac{5}{7} = \dfrac{b}{42}$

4. $\dfrac{8}{9} = \dfrac{p}{63}$

$n =$ _____ $x =$ _____ $b =$ _____ $p =$ _____

Use equal ratios to solve each problem.

5. The Dollar-Mart grocery store sells 6 bars of soap for $1.00. How many bars of soap can a customer buy with $9.00?

6. Kelsey's soccer team scored 5 points in 2 games. At this rate, how many points will the team score in 16 games?

7. The O'Neil family is driving 60 miles per hour. If they continue to drive at this speed, how many miles will they drive in 4 hours?

Write quotation marks where they are needed in the paragraph.

Our Special Spring Program

Holly Street Middle School will hold a spring program next month. I will be the

announcer for the program. I will say, The drama team is proud to present a

famous story about a young woman who was too curious. After the drama team's

performance, Mr. Graham's class will recite The Cloud by Percy Bysshe Shelley. Ms.

Carrol's class will sing The Ashe Grove.

DAY 8

Read each situation. Then, answer the question to predict what will happen next.

Sally Ann is 80 years old. She lives in a house with a small, fenced yard. She decided to adopt a dog to keep her company. Sally Ann went to the animal shelter and narrowed her choice to two dogs. The first was a large, one-year-old retriever. He had a lot of energy and was accustomed to running on acres of land. The second dog was a small, three-year-old spaniel. He was very calm and knew how to use a doggy door to go out into the yard.

8. Which dog do you think Sally Ann will choose? Why? _____

_____

_____

Harry's weekend was busy. He spent Friday night at Roberto's house, and they stayed up late watching movies. Harry left early the next morning for baseball practice. He was exhausted when he finally returned home, but he helped his mom get ready for the party they were hosting that evening. When all of the preparations were finished, Harry went to his room and eyed his bed. He still had three hours before the party began.

9. What do you think will happen next? Why? _____

_____

_____

Pretend that people on Earth have finally learned how to live on other planets. Which planet would you most like to live on other than Earth? Why did you choose that planet? You can use some research materials to help you decide your answer. Use another sheet of paper if you need more space.

_____

_____

_____

_____

_____

FACTOID: The sun's diameter is approximately 870,000 miles (1,400,000 km).

Use cross multiplication to solve each proportion.

1. $\dfrac{5}{2} = \dfrac{10}{m}$

2. $\dfrac{3}{a} = \dfrac{9}{3}$

3. $\dfrac{12}{d} = \dfrac{3}{1}$

4. $\dfrac{7}{n} = \dfrac{2}{4}$

5. $\dfrac{p}{15} = \dfrac{6}{5}$

6. $\dfrac{14}{21} = \dfrac{j}{3}$

7. $\dfrac{120}{30} = \dfrac{s}{5}$

8. $\dfrac{y}{18} = \dfrac{3}{6}$

9. $\dfrac{100}{20} = \dfrac{5}{r}$

10. $\dfrac{24}{k} = \dfrac{8}{12}$

11. $\dfrac{g}{15} = \dfrac{8}{5}$

12. $\dfrac{5}{5} = \dfrac{7}{t}$

Rewrite each sentence. Add single quotation marks where needed.

13. Phillip said, "I read the article Bike Safety by Mike B. Helmet."

_____

14. "Would you play Moonlight Sonata on the piano?" asked Sadie.

_____

15. "My essay Life in Antarctica is due tomorrow," explained Ramsey.

_____

16. Maja said, "My favorite poem is The Road Not Taken."

_____

17. "We have to read the chapter titled Nighttime again," Marla complained.

_____

DAY 9

Read the poem. Then, answer the questions.

Emily Dickinson

During her lifetime, Emily Dickinson published only 7 of the approximately 1,800 poems that she wrote. Most of her poems were published posthumously, or after her death. Today, Dickinson is known for her unusual use of capital letters and punctuation, vivid imagery, slant rhyme, and broken meter. She did not give her poems titles. Instead, Dickinson's poems are often organized in chronological order and assigned a number based on when scholars think each poem was written.

254
"Hope" is the thing with feathers –
That perches in the soul –
And sings the tune without the words –
And never stops – at all –

And sweetest – in the Gale – is heard –
And sore must be the storm –
That could abash the little Bird –
That kept so many warm –

I've heard it in the chilliest land –
And on the strangest Sea –
Yet, never, in Extremity –
It asked a crumb – of Me.

18. To what does Emily Dickinson compare hope? _____

19. What do you think Dickinson means when she writes that hope is ". . . sweetest –
     in the Gale. . . "? _____

     _____

20. When words sound the same but do not rhyme exactly, they are called slant
     rhymes. Write one pair of slant rhymes from the poem.

     _____ / _____

FITNESS FLASH: Hop on your right foot for 30 seconds.

* See page ii.

Find the radius of each circle.

1.

2.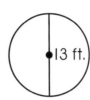

3.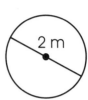

4.

_____   _____   _____   _____

Find the diameter of each circle.

5.

6.

7.

8.

_____   _____   _____   _____

Write hyphens where they are needed in each sentence.

9. The sports loving fans did not seem to notice the freezing temperatures.

10. Ilene made her mother in law a chocolate cake for her birthday.

11. The store has forty four electric fans in stock.

12. Mikacia saw twenty one meteors in the pitch black sky.

13. Fifty eight people waited two hours in the late afternoon drizzle for tickets to see the movie.

Write two sentences. Use at least one hyphen in each sentence.

14. _____

15. _____

DAY 10

Read each paragraph. Circle the accessory that each paragraph describes. Then, underline the context clues that helped you choose your answer.

16. Sharon was looking for something to carry on her business trip. She wanted it to be large enough to hold her money, glasses, and address book. She preferred that it would have a shoulder strap and match the clothes she was taking.

   A. wallet   B. purse
   C. suitcase   D. backpack

17. Sharon stopped at a store. She told the salesperson where she was going and what clothes she was taking. She explained that the most important thing was that she be comfortable while standing all day and demonstrating her product. Sharon sat down to try on some of the things the salesperson brought her.

   A. hat   B. shoes
   C. luggage   D. belt

Label the diagram of Earth's interior using the terms from the word bank. Use reference resources if you need help.

asthenosphere	inner core	mantle
crust	lithosphere	outer core

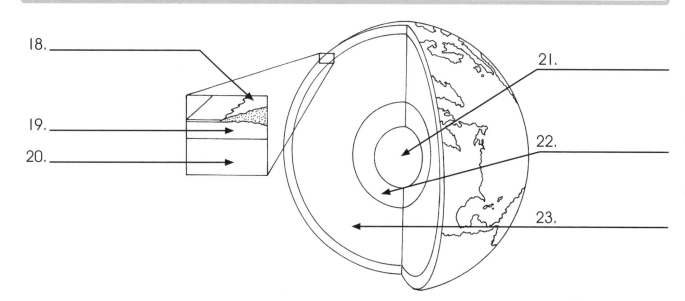

18. _____
19. _____
20. _____
21. _____
22. _____
23. _____

CHARACTER CHECK: Make a list of five ways that you can show integrity.

DAY 11

Find the circumference of each circle. Use 3.14 for pi (π).

1.
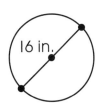
16 in.

2.

18 km

3.
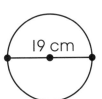
19 cm

4.

8 ft.

_____ _____ _____ _____

5.
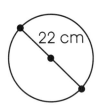
22 cm

6.

5 m

7.

11 cm

8.

14 in.

_____ _____ _____ _____

Write en dashes and em dashes where they are needed in each sentence.

9. The appointments available are 12:00 P.M. 4:00 P.M.

10. The assignment for tomorrow is to read pages 24 36 carefully.

11. The Chicago New York flight lasts less than two hours.

12. We go to great lengths often far beyond our normal limitations to win!

13. If I only needed to read chapters 2 4, I would be finished by now.

DAY 11

Circle the letter next to the word that completes each analogy.

14. Chapter : book :: act : _____.

    A. novel   B. comedy   C. play   D. sitcom

15. Thrifty : miserly :: smart : _____.

    A. cheap   B. foolish   C. gullible   D. brilliant

16. Waltz : dance :: oak : _____.

    A. acorn   B. tree   C. pine   D. tango

17. Reveal : divulge :: hide : _____.

    A. discover   B. imagine   C. conceal   D. inform

18. Stiff : flexible :: empty : _____.

    A. low   B. rigid   C. full   D. elastic

A fault is a break in Earth's crust where pieces of the crust slip past each other. There are three main kinds of faults: *normal*, *reverse*, and *strike-slip*. Label each diagram by writing the type of fault it represents. Use reference resources if you need help.

19. This type of fault is caused by tension forces.

    _____

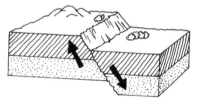

20. This type of fault is caused by shear forces.

    _____

21. This type of fault is caused by compression forces.

    _____

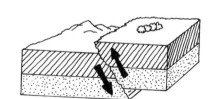

FACTOID: The world's oldest known living tree, a conifer in Sweden, has a root system that has been growing for more than 9,500 years.

Find the area and the perimeter of each figure.

1.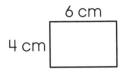
6 cm
4 cm

A = _____ P = _____

2.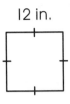
12 in.

A = _____ P = _____

3.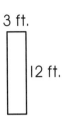
3 ft.
12 ft.

A = _____ P = _____

4.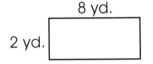
8 yd.
2 yd.

A = _____ P = _____

5.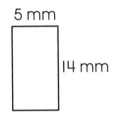
5 mm
14 mm

A = _____ P = _____

6.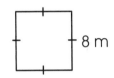
8 m

A = _____ P = _____

Write em dashes where they are needed in the paragraph.

Woeful Woofer

Woofer that silly dog is home again. I called actually, whistled for Woofer to come to dinner. Usually, he runs into the kitchen, but the house was quiet. I didn't know where he could be. I was searching for Woofer when Carol my older sister came home from school. When I told her that Woofer was missing, she helped me look in every room even under the beds. We couldn't find Woofer. Carol asked Mrs. Linden the retired teacher next door if she had seen him. Then, Nicholas Carol's friend walked up the street with Woofer trotting behind him.

Read the passage. Then, answer the questions.

Giant Superstars

In December 2000, two giant pandas arrived in the United States from China. The pair was delivered to the National Zoo in Washington, D.C. Their names are Mei Xiang (may SHONG) and Tian Tian (t-YEN t-YEN). In July 2005, Mei Xiang and Tian Tian had a cub. When he was 100 days old, he was given the name Tai Shan (tie SHON), which means "peaceful mountain."

The pandas' exhibit has both indoor and outdoor areas where they can roam freely. Because pandas dislike hot, humid weather, the outdoor habitat is air-conditioned. Visitors can watch the pandas graze on bamboo shoots, apples, carrots, and special biscuits.

Giant pandas are rare and have always been popular in zoos. Only about 1,600 remain in the wild. They live in the mountain forests in China. Pandas face dangers from poachers and the destruction of their habitats. The Chinese government has made a tradition of loaning or giving pandas to other countries as a symbol of friendship. This new pair of pandas is on loan to the United States. The United States must pay a $1 million per year "rental fee" for Mei Xiang and Tian Tian.

7. What types of food can the National Zoo's visitors watch the pandas eat?

   _____

8. Why do you think giant pandas are among the most popular attractions at zoos throughout the world? _____

   _____

9. Describe the pandas' exhibit at the National Zoo. _____

   _____

   _____

10. Why does the Chinese government loan or give pandas to other countries?

   _____

   _____

FITNESS FLASH: Do 10 jumping jacks.

* See page ii.

Find the area of each figure.

1.

   12 cm

   9 cm

   A = _____ cm²

2.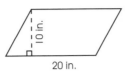

   10 in.

   20 in.

   A = _____ in.²

3.

   6 ft.

   6 ft.

   A = _____ ft.²

4.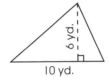

   6 yd.

   10 yd.

   A = _____ yd.²

5.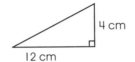

   4 cm

   12 cm

   A = _____ cm²

6.

   7 cm

   5 cm

   A = _____ cm²

Write semicolons and commas where they are needed in each sentence.

7.   Marcy forgot to bring a suitcase Mindy remembered.

8.   So far this month, John has traveled to Jackson Mississippi Tallahassee Florida
     and Nashville Tennessee.

9.   Casey looked forward to the weekend his uncle was coming to visit.

10. Jonah's class made lunch for Mr. Burns the custodian Mrs. Fry the head cook
     and Miss Bookman the librarian.

11. Sometimes we stay late after practice however we leave when the coach
     goes home.

DAY 13

Circle the letter next to the word that completes each analogy.

12. Sour : lemon :: sweet : _____.

    A.   cake   B.   water   C.   flowers   D.   rice

13. Vine : grapes :: tree : _____.

    A.   bird   B.   nuts   C.   lumber   D.   swing

14. Sip : drink :: chew : _____.

    A.   food   B.   water   C.   dirt   D.   fork

15. Vegetable : corn :: candy : _____.

    A.   yellow   B.   wrapper   C.   eat   D.   peppermint

16. Song : songwriter :: book : _____.

    A.   author   B.   person   C.   singer   D.   agent

Perseverance Interview

Perseverance means not giving up, even if something is difficult to do. Talk with family members about perseverance. Encourage them to tell you about people they know who demonstrate the quality of perseverance.

Select one person that your family mentioned. Contact this person and ask if you can conduct an interview. Ask specific questions to help you understand the challenges the person overcame to be successful. After the interview, choose one of the options below as a way of sharing your appreciation to the person you interviewed.

A. Write the person a note highlighting what you learned and how the person's story of persevering affected you personally.

B. Make a poster that highlights the person's accomplishments. Include an appropriate slogan that you will be able to use in your own life.

FACTOID: The Pacific barreleye fish has a transparent head.

Find the volume of each cube.

1.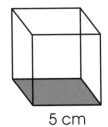

5 cm

V = _____

2.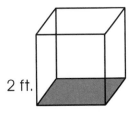

2 ft.

V = _____

3.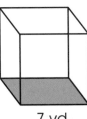

7 yd.

V = _____

4.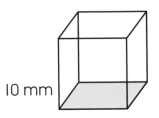

10 mm

V = _____

5.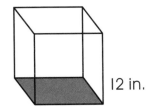

12 in.

V = _____

6.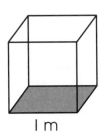

1 m

V = _____

Write colons where they are needed in each phrase or sentence.

7. At 3 00 P.M., everyone in class needs to take the following items to the auditorium a pencil, an eraser, and a notebook.

8. To Whom It May Concern

9. I need a few things to make a new recipe corn, tomatoes, onions, black beans, and cilantro.

Write a sentence that includes a direct quotation. The sentence has been started for you. Remember to add a colon where it is needed.

One of my favorite songs begins with _____

_____

_____

_____

DAY 14

Jayla, Judy, Chuck, and Bill have different jobs: lifeguard, lawyer, pilot, and professor. Each drives a different type of vehicle: truck, motorcycle, bike, or car. Use the chart and the clues to determine each person's job and vehicle.

- Jayla is afraid of flying.
- Judy gets to her office on a vehicle that has two wheels.
- For Chuck's job, he often passes through two or three states each day.
- The person who is the lifeguard also drives the truck.
- A man rides a bike to his job.
- A man needs a large trunk to bring graded papers back and forth to work.

	Lifeguard	Lawyer	Pilot	Professor
Jayla				
Judy				
Chuck				
Bill				

Imagine that a family from another country is visiting your town or city. What should they see? Where should they go? Create a five-day itinerary for the family that explores your town's or city's landmarks and attractions. Use another sheet of paper if you need more space.

_____

_____

_____

_____

_____

FITNESS FLASH: Jog in place for 30 seconds.

* See page ii.

Find the volume of each rectangular prism.

1.
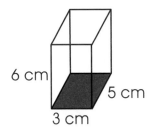
6 ft. 5 ft. 8 ft.

V = _____

2.
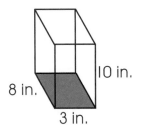
10 in. 8 in. 3 in.

V = _____

3.
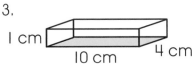
1 cm 10 cm 4 cm

V = _____

4.
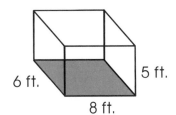
6 cm 5 cm 3 cm

V = _____

5.
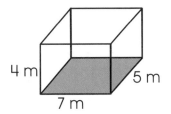
4 m 5 m 7 m

V = _____

6.
9 yd. 5 yd. 13 yd.

V = _____

Write the abbreviation for each word. Add periods when needed.

7. Mister _____

8. ounce _____

9. yard _____

10. Company _____

11. Captain _____

12. inch _____

13. Association _____

14. Avenue _____

15. et cetera _____

16. Doctor _____

17. Miss _____

18. feet _____

19. Street _____

20. pound _____

21. Junior _____

22. Incorporated _____

23. Senior _____

24. Boulevard _____

25. United States _____

26. General _____

27. Professor _____

Read the passage. Then, answer the questions.

Matthew Henson

The man stood in the cold, white world, waiting for the other sleds to arrive. Suddenly, he realized that he was standing farther north than any other person in history.

The explorer was an African American man named Matthew Henson. He was on an expedition with Robert Peary to the North Pole, but it was not the first time Henson had made this journey. He had worked for Peary for more than 20 years. He had been with Peary all of the times the explorer had tried to make it to the North Pole and failed. In 1908, Peary decided to try one last time. He insisted that Henson go with him.

Matthew Henson learned a great deal from his work with Peary. He knew how to survive in the Arctic. He became friends with the native inhabitants and learned their language. He used their information to help him plan the final expedition. Henson's plans with Peary were precise. The team put **caches**, or stockpiles, of food in igloos along the trail. They would use this food on their way back after they ran out of supplies from the sleds. Henson was the best driver of the dog teams, so he took the lead and broke the trail. This time, the team was successful. On April 6, 1909, Matthew Henson stood with Peary and their crew at the northernmost place on Earth.

28. What does the word *caches* mean in the passage? _____

29. Number the events in the order they happened.

    _____ Robert Peary says that he will make one more trip to the Arctic.

    _____ Matthew Henson starts working for Robert Peary.

    _____ Matthew Henson carefully plans the final trip to the North Pole.

    _____ Matthew Henson stands at the North Pole for the first time.

30. When did Henson reach the northernmost place on Earth?

    _____

31. Where did Henson get some of his information when planning their trips?

    _____

> **CHARACTER CHECK: In the evening, discuss with an adult how you demonstrated honesty today.**

Use a protractor to measure each angle. Then, write the measurement and classify the angle as *acute*, *right*, or *obtuse*.

1.

2.

3.

_____ _____

4.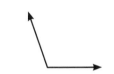

5.

6.

_____ _____ _____

Rewrite each sentence to correct the double negative.

7. Sidney couldn't do nothing with her hair.

    _____

8. Todd didn't have no second thoughts about the decision he made.

    _____

9. No, Celia didn't see nobody else at the market.

    _____

10. Kevin could not never see the road because of the heavy snow.

    _____

11. Mia hasn't received no mail in more than a week.

    _____

12. I didn't borrow none of the movies from Toni.

    _____

DAY 16

Five words that are often associated with reading and writing have been broken into syllables. Read each clue. Assemble the answer using syllables from the box.

a	mag	news	pe	per
rec	vel	pa	ope	zine
a	ry	en	di	i

13. tells what is happening each day _____

14. read for fun or information _____

15. a place to write secrets _____

16. what a letter goes into before it is mailed _____

17. followed when cooking _____

Write the letter of each term next to its definition.

18. _____ water in the form of rain, snow, sleet, or hail falls from clouds onto Earth's surface   A. condensation

19. _____ the process by which clouds form as water vapor cools and changes into liquid water droplets   B. evaporation

20. _____ how water soaks into the ground   C. infiltration

21. _____ water that flows across land and into streams, rivers, or oceans   D. precipitation

22. _____ the process by which water on Earth's surface changes from liquid to water vapor   E. runoff

23. _____ evaporation of water into the atmosphere from the leaves and stems of plants   F. transpiration

FACTOID: The average summer temperature in Antarctica is 35.6°F (2°C).

Find the measure of the missing angle in each triangle. Then, classify the triangle as *acute*, *right*, or *obtuse*.

1.
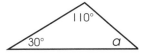
110°
30°   a

a = _____

_____

2.
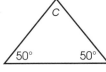
c
50°   50°

c = _____

_____

3.
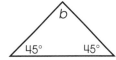
b
45°   45°

b = _____

_____

4.
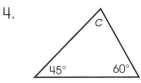
c
45°   60°

c = _____

_____

5.
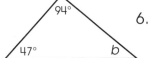
94°
47°   b

b = _____

_____

6.
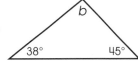
81°
53°   a

a = _____

_____

7.

b
38°   45°

b = _____

_____

8.
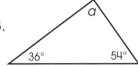
a
36°   54°

a = _____

_____

Write the letter of each sentence next to the sentence that explains its meaning.

9. A. Stop that girl Meg.
    B. Stop that girl, Meg.

_____ You are asking someone to stop a girl named Meg.

_____ You are asking Meg to stop a girl.

10. A. I will ask, Jade.
    B. I will ask Jade.

_____ You are telling Jade you will ask someone a question.

_____ You will ask Jade a question.

11. A. Help them push Kendall.
    B. Help them push, Kendall.

_____ You are asking Kendall to help others push something.

_____ You are asking someone to help push Kendall, possibly on a sled or swing.

12. A. Call her Rebecca.
    B. Call her, Rebecca.

_____ You are telling Rebecca to call another girl.

_____ You are telling someone to call a girl by the name Rebecca.

DAY 17

Circle the letter next to the answer for each question about using a dictionary.

13. The guide words are *justice* and *juvenile*. Locate the word *just*.

    A. previous page   B. this page   C. next page

14. The guide words are *wonder* and *woodsy*. Which word is not on the page?

    A. wood   B. won   C. woodchuck

15. Look at the guide words. On which page will you find the word *frugal*?

    A. froth–fruit   B. fuji–funny   C. full–fumble

16. The guide words are *yearbook* and *yellow jacket*. Which word is on the page?

    A. yellow   B. year   C. yelp

17. Which word will be last on the page?

    A. payable   B. payee   C. pay

18. Which word will be first on the page?

    A. halfpenny   B. half   C. halfway

19. The guide words are *sealant* and *seatrain*. Which word is not on the page?

    A. seat   B. seem   C. search

20. The guide words are *applesauce* and *apply*. Which word is on the page?

    A. appreciate   B. application   C. apple

High-Knees Drill

Have you ever wondered how a football player gains the speed and agility to run through players and score? He regularly does the high-knees drill! Begin by placing five soft objects in a row, approximately five feet apart. Then, with knees high and eyes straight ahead, run full speed over each object. For an added challenge, try holding a ball while running. Set monthly goals to increase the number of times that you do this drill and watch as your speed and endurance improve.

FITNESS FLASH: Hop on your right foot for 30 seconds.

* See page ii.

Use the diagram to answer each question.

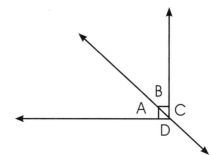

1. m∠A + m∠B = _____

These are called _____ angles.

2. m∠D + m∠_____ = 180°

These are called _____ angles.

Use the diagram to answer each question.

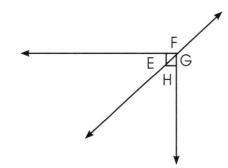

3. If m∠H = 43°,

m∠E = _____

m∠G = _____

m∠F = _____

4. If m∠G = 132°,

m∠H = _____

m∠E = _____

m∠F = _____

Draw three lines beneath each letter that should be capitalized in the paragraph.

Fascinating Reading

I read the latest issue of *Around the World* at the dentist's office today. First, I read an article about the absence of land plants during the cambrian period of the paleozoic era. Then, I read an article by Ned Clive of the world Relief society about the indonesian earthquake. I had just started an article about planets when the hygienist called me. Next, i want to read the article about hiking trails in the Pacific northwest.

DAY 18

Read the passage. Then, answer the questions.

Ancient Egypt

Egypt was unified under pharaohs, or rulers, about 5,000 years ago. Egyptians built pyramids to honor pharaohs and house treasures, such as gold and jewels. Archaeologists are not sure how these great buildings were constructed, but they do know that it took many people to lift the large, heavy stones into place. The Ancient Egyptians wrote on paper made from papyrus, a plant that grew along the banks of the Nile River. They wrote with hieroglyphics, a written language that uses pictures. Archaeologists could not read the Egyptian writing until they found a special rock called the Rosetta Stone. It had the same passage written in three languages, one of which was hieroglyphics. Because people could read the other languages on the stone, they could translate the hieroglyphics. Then, archaeologists could finally begin to read what the Egyptians had written about their culture.

5. What is the main idea of this passage?

    A. Pharaohs collected treasures, such as gold and jewels.

    B. Egyptians had a lot to say about their culture.

    C. The ancient Egyptians built pyramids and wrote in hieroglyphics.

6. Who were the pharaohs? _____

    _____

7. Why were the pyramids built? _____

    _____

8. What is papyrus? _____

    _____

9. How are hieroglyphics different from English writing? _____

    _____

    _____

> **FACTOID:** The most active muscles in the human body are the muscles that move the eyes. They contract more than 100,000 times a day.

Look at the 3 x 3 arrangements of dots below. How many squares can be made from 9 dots if you use the dots to mark their corners? Use the grids below to show all of the squares that you can make. Hint: There are more than 5 squares.

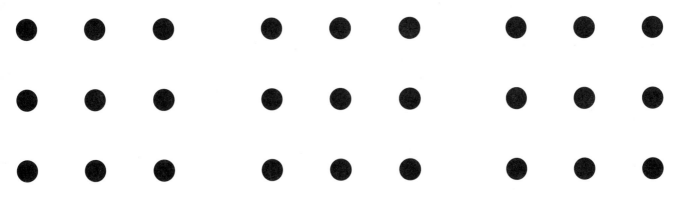

Add or remove punctuation where it is needed in the paragraph.

School Newspaper Survey

Our school newspaper (*The Bobcat Times* took a survey last week The results were published today. The first survey question was What's your favorite movie. Two fifths of the students preferred big surprise—*March of the Penguins*. The girls favorite film was *The Incredibles* the boys favorite was *Harry Potter and the Chamber of Secrets*. The second survey question was What's your favorite poem?" The sixth grade students' favorites were the following Toothpaste by Michael Rosen "The Honey Pot" by Alan Riddell and Mean Song" by Eve Merriam.

DAY 19

Write the best resource to use for each task.

1. locate the pronunciation of *scrivener* _____

2. find a different word for *excellent* _____

3. determine the continent(s) that border(s) Asia _____

4. find more than 15 definitions for *run* _____

5. find the definition of *scalene* in your math book_____

6. locate the pages in your science book that refer to plant roots _____

7. gather information about castles for your class report _____

8. find the definition of *genealogy* in your social studies book _____

9. label the countries of South America on a map _____

10. find seven facts about roller coasters _____

If you could add a holiday to the calendar that everyone in the country would celebrate, what would it be, when would it be, and how would it be celebrated? Use a separate piece of paper if you need more space.

_____

_____

_____

_____

_____

_____

_____

_____

FITNESS FLASH: Hop on your left foot 10 times.

* See page ii.

Solve each problem. Draw and label your answers in the space provided.

1. Phoebe has 9 rocks. She puts the rocks into 3 boxes. Each box has 1 more rock than the previous box. How many rocks are in each box?

2. Alyssa has 4 boxes that contain a total of 30 seeds. Three of the boxes contain the same number of seeds. The fourth box contains the sum of the other 3 boxes. How many seeds are in each box?

Writing is more interesting when a variety of sentence structures are used. Write a sentence to fit each description.

3. Write a sentence with a simple subject and simple predicate with adjectives, articles, and adverbs.

    _____

4. Write a sentence with a direct object and an indirect object.

    _____

5. Write a sentence with two prepositional phrases.

    _____

6. Write a sentence with a compound subject and/or verb.

    _____

DAY 20

Circle the letter next to the best resource to use for each task.

7. In which reference book would you find the best map of your country?

   A. dictionary   B. atlas   C. thesaurus

8. In which reference book would you find the definition of the word *congregate*?

   A. dictionary   B. atlas   C. encyclopedia

9. In which reference book would you find information about the history and economy of Honduras?

   A. dictionary   B. thesaurus   C. encyclopedia

10. In which reference book would you find what time the sun will rise tomorrow?

    A. dictionary   B. almanac   C. atlas

Write the word from the word bank that matches each description.

demand	profit	inflation	scarcity	supply

11. the amount of a good or service that people are willing and able to purchase at a given price _____

12. an increase in the average cost of goods and services _____

13. the amount of a product available for sale _____

14. when there are not enough goods and services available to meet demand

    _____

15. The amount of money that a company makes after paying for all supplies, resources, and overhead costs _____

CHARACTER CHECK: Do something thoughtful for a friend or family member today, such as helping fold laundry or taking out the trash.

The Doppler Effect

Why does the sound of a buzzer change as the buzzer moves closer or farther away?

Have you noticed that the sound of a car as it approaches is different from its sound after it passes? This is because the sound waves produced by the car have a higher frequency as the car approaches you and a lower frequency as the car travels away from you. This is called the Doppler effect. In this activity, you will demonstrate the Doppler effect.

Materials:
- small buzzer
- audio recorder
- plastic tub of water
- pebble

Procedure:

Hold the buzzer in front of the audio recorder. Turn on the buzzer and record the sound. Play the recording to make sure that it sounds the same as the buzzer's original sound.

Record the buzzer's sound again. This time, move the buzzer toward and away from the recorder several times. Play the recording and listen to how the buzzer's pitch (the highness or lowness of a sound) changes during the recording.

1. Describe the difference between the first recording and the second recording.

   _____

   _____

Drop the pebble into the plastic tub of water. Watch the ripples in the water. These ripples show what happens when something makes a sound and the air vibrates. The sound waves spread in every direction, similar to the water ripples. These ripples look like the sound waves that the buzzer made when you held it still in front of the recorder.

Drag your fingers across the water's surface. These ripples look like the sound waves when you moved the buzzer toward and away from the recorder. The sound waves near the buzzer are closer, which makes the sound's pitch higher. When the buzzer is farther from the recorder, the sound waves are farther apart and the pitch is lower.

2. Describe how the ripples created by dropping the pebble into the water are

   different from the ripples created by dragging your fingers across the water.

   _____

   _____

BONUS

Solar "Still" Works

What is a solar still? How does a solar still work?

Solar energy is a renewable resource because, unlike energy resources, such as oil and coal, it is quickly replenished. Renewable energy can help solve environmental problems, such as drought. In some coastal areas where there are low levels of freshwater for drinking and farming, people use a device called a solar still to create freshwater. In this activity, you will create a solar still and discover how it works.

Materials:
- clear glass measuring cup
- teaspoon
- large plastic cup
- plastic wrap
- small rock
- water
- salt
- small paper cup
- rubber band

Procedure:

Fill the measuring cup with 8 ounces (0.24 L) of water and 1–2 teaspoons (4.9–9.8 mL) of salt. Stir the water and salt until the salt dissolves. Dip your finger into the water and taste it.

Pour about 2 ounces (1/4 cup) of salt water into the large plastic cup. Place the small paper cup inside the large cup so that it floats. Then, cover the large cup with plastic wrap and secure it tightly with the rubber band. Place the small rock in the middle of the plastic wrap so that it sags slightly. Do not allow the rock to touch the salt water or rip the plastic wrap.

Place the cups in a sunny location and check them after a few hours. Record your observations on the lines. After a few days, check the cups by removing the plastic wrap. Record your observations. Dip your finger into the small cup's water and taste it.

Observations:

1. How was solar energy used in this activity?_____

   _____

   _____

2. How might this method be used on a larger scale?_____

   _____

   _____

Straight to the Source!

What primary sources do you create each day?

A primary source provides information about an event from someone who was present when that event occurred. Letters, photographs, diaries, artifacts, and news footage are examples of primary sources. You probably create several primary sources every day, sometimes without even realizing it!

1. List five activities you participated in during the last 24 hours. Beside each activity, write any evidence, such as cash register receipts, that you left behind.

    _____

    _____

    _____

    _____

    _____

2. List any personal records that you created, such as e-mail messages, a blog entry, or a photograph. _____

    _____

    _____

3. Would your activities be mentioned in a primary source, such as a friend's journal entry, a government record, or the local newspaper? If so, list the sources that would mention your activities. _____

    _____

4. Look at your responses for questions 1–3. Judging from this evidence, what conclusions or inferences could future historians make about your day?

    _____

    _____

5. Why is it important to create written records? _____

    _____

BONUS

The Age of Exploration

During the Age of Exploration, European countries sent explorers to find new trade routes, look for gold, and establish new colonies. Write the surname of each explorer from the word bank to complete the crossword puzzle.

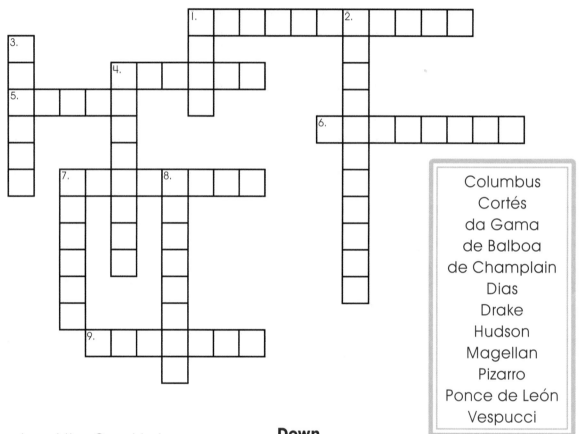

Word Bank:
Columbus
Cortés
da Gama
de Balboa
de Champlain
Dias
Drake
Hudson
Magellan
Pizarro
Ponce de León
Vespucci

Across

1. explored the Great Lakes, Samuel _____

4. first European to reach India by sea, Vasco _____

5. first Englishman to sail around the world, Sir Frances _____

6. traveled to the West Indies and South America for Spain and Portugal, Amerigo _____

7. made four voyages to the West Indies, Christopher _____

9. made contact with the Inca Empire, Francisco _____

Down

1. first European to sail around Africa, Bartolomeu _____

2. explored Florida, Juan _____

3. explored a river and bay in North America, later named for him, Henry _____

4. crossed Panama; sighted the Pacific Ocean, Vasco _____

7. conquered the Aztec Kingdom, Hernando _____

8. planned and led the first voyage to sail around the world, Ferdinand _____

Renaissance Men and Women

Write each person's name beneath the correct heading. Use reference resources if you need help. Then, research one person from the list. Write three facts about the person you chose on the lines.

The term *renaissance* refers to a rebirth or a rediscovery. The Renaissance marked a continuation of learning and creativity of the Classical Age. Hallmarks of the Renaissance included a celebration of the individual rather than the group, interest in the ideas of ancient Greece and Rome, enjoyment of worldly pleasures, and the rejection of the simple life of feudal times.

Blaise Pascal	Catherine dé Medici	Dante Alighieri
Elizabeth I	Galileo Galilei	Geoffrey Chaucer
Henry VII	Thomas More	Isaac Newton
Johannes Gutenberg	John Calvin	Leonardo da Vinci
Martin Luther	Michelangelo	Nicolaus Copernicus
Peter Henlein	Raphael Santi	William Shakespeare

1. artists

   _____

   _____

   _____

2. scientists

   _____

   _____

   _____

3. writers

   _____

   _____

   _____

4. religious leaders

   _____

   _____

   _____

5. royalty

   _____

   _____

   _____

6. inventors

   _____

   _____

   _____

_____

_____

_____

_____

_____

BONUS

Take It Outside!

Go for a walk around your neighborhood. Take a pen and a notebook with you. Periodically pause and write notes about what you have done, seen, and heard. Review your notes when you return home. Then, write a 50-word summary about your walk. Next, edit your summary to 30 words. Be sure to keep the main ideas. Can you edit your writing to a 20- or 10-word summary?

Contact the water treatment facility for your community. Find out when tours are offered. Schedule a time with a family member to take the tour. Bring a pen and a notebook. Highlight the steps in the process of treating the water for community consumption. After the tour, make a chart showing the process. Share the procedural chart with friends. Also, write a note to the water treatment facility, highlighting what you learned and thanking them for their time spent giving you the tour.

Talk with a family member about scheduling a time to go to a local sporting event. Think of the many people it takes to organize and host a game or match. When the date arrives, bring a pen and a notebook with you. Pay attention to the various people who work at the event, as well as the participants and spectators. After attending the game, write a paragraph about the people who were there and the roles they played.